# BACK ROADS TO FAR TOWNS

# BACK ROADS
# TO FAR TOWNS

*Bashō's OKU-NO-HOSOMICHI*

*with a translation and notes by*
CID CORMAN *and* KAMAIKE SUSUMU

*illustrated by*
HAYAKAWA IKUTADA

THE ECCO PRESS

THE ECCO PRESS
100 West Broad Street
Hopewell, New Jersey 08525
Published simultaneously in Canada by
Penguin Books Canada Ltd., Ontario
Printed in the United States of America

Library of Congress Cataloging-in-Publication Data
Bashō, Matsuo, 1644–1694
Back roads to far towns
translations and notes by Cid Corman and Kamaike Susumu
translation is of Bashō's oku-no-hosomichi
introduction by Robert Hass
ISBN 0-88001-467-9 (paperback)

9 8 7 6 5 4 3 2 1

FIRST ECCO EDITION

# TABLE OF CONTENTS

# BASHŌ'S NARROW PATH AND CID CORMAN'S BACK ROADS
## by Robert Hass

In the fall of 1955, the young Jack Kerouac, hitchhiking and hopping freights from Mexico City to San Francisco, discovered Buddhism and began to have visions of himself as a wandering holy man. Later, in *The Dharma Bums,* he recast the vision in a box car rattling through the San Joaquin Valley, his companion a rheumy old man expert at cadging free rides on the Southern Pacific, the last of the Depression hoboes brought into conjunction with the first of the post-war Beats: "I believe that I was an old-time bhikku in modern clothes wandering the world (usually the immense triangular arc of New York to Mexico City to San Francisco) in order to turn the wheel of the True Meaning, or Dharma, and gain merit for myself as a future Buddha (Awakener) and as a future Hero in Paradise." Arriving in North Beach, Kerouac hooked up with his Columbia University classmate Allen Ginsberg in Berkeley, who introduced him to a graduate student in East Asian languages named Gary Snyder. In the novel, published in 1958, Snyder became Japhy Ryder, who "learned Chinese and Japanese and became an Oriental scholar and discovered the greatest Dharma Bums of them all, the Zen lunatics of China and Japan."

By the time the novel was published Gary Snyder had moved to Kyoto to receive Zen Buddhist training at its source, and Kerouac had become, destructively for him, the hero to a generation. Lots of the young had been taken by that moment in the book when Japhy and Ray Smith, the stand-in for Kerouac, are resting from a long hike in the Sierra Nevada, quoting to each other recently discovered poems and koans from their favorite wise men and imagining the spiritual traditions of Buddhism and Taoism taking root in America. *Tao* means "way," or "road"; it's no accident that Bashō's great work, *Oku-no-ho-somichi* might be translated literally, "the back country's narrow path (or narrow lanes)." "I see a vision of a great rucksack revolution," Kerouac wrote, "thousands or even millions of young Americans wandering around with their rucksacks, going up the mountains to pray, making children laugh and old men glad . . . Zen lunatics who go about writing poems and also by being kind and by strange unexpected acts giving vision of freedom to everybody and all living creatures."

When Kerouac and Snyder were meeting in San Francisco, a young Cid Corman, recently graduated from Tufts University and writing poetry, was in New York collaborating with another young poet, Leroi Jones, later Amiri Baraka, on a magazine of new American poetry called *Origin*. Jones would soon start his own magazine and give it a title drawn from one of the central ideas in Bashō's aesthetic, *yūgen* which means, roughly, "deep, mysterious, and graceful." Corman published many of the young writers who were trying to find a new way for American poetry, including Ginsberg and Snyder. Just about the time *The Dharma Bums* was published, and the young were hitchhiking around the country with it in their backpacks, using it as a handbook on turning yourself from a beatnik into a hippie, Corman received a Fulbright Scholarship and went to Kyoto, where he continued to write poems, married a Japanese woman, founded Origin Press to publish work of the new generation, and with his wife ran an ice cream shop from the store front of his not deeply lucrative publishing business. At about this time he also began to study and translate, with Kamaike Susume, the greatest of all Japanese books of spiritual wandering, Bashō's *Narrow Road*.

Corman called his version *Back Roads to Far Towns*, I think, because he was determined to resist the orientalizing, the stately and faintly mysterious tone that had become a cliché of so much translation of Asian literature into English. The excitement of this book, its deep accomplishment, is that he and his co-translator really do manage to make Bashō seem entirely new without making him over into an American. The clipped notational style of the prose may sound a bit like Kerouac or the on-the-run poetics of Ginsberg and Snyder, but it also catches the immediacy of Bashō's own style:

> In the demesne of Yamagata, the mountain temple called
> Ryushakuji. Founded by Jikaku Daishi, an unusually well-kept

quiet place. "You must go and see it, people urged, from here, off back toward Obanazawa, about seven *li*. Sun not down yet. Reserved space at dormitory at bottom, then climbed to the temple on the ridge. This old earth and stone smooth moss, and on the rocks temple doors locked, no sound. Climbed along edges of and crept over boulders, worshiped at temples, penetrating scene, profound quietness, heart/mind clear.

> quiet
> into rock absorbing
> cicada sounds

As he worked, Corman was a beginning student of Japanese literature, and his translation is so alive because his interest wasn't merely academic. He was transforming into English a tradition his own culture needed, and he had found a style that engaged the most interesting new writing of his own time. Most great translations have that quality: they are acts of discovery, both of the original text and of the language that the writer is working in. Before long the Grossman edition of *Back Roads To Far Towns* had entered the backpacks of the young along with *The Dharma Bums* and Snyder's translations of one of Bashō's teachers, the T'ang Zen Buddhist poet-hermit Han Shan.

That moment has come and gone. But it has left its trace. There are, as I write, more practicing Buddhists in the United States than there are Presbyterians, and Americans today know much more about the traditions of Chinese and Japanese literature. And there is lately a revival of interest among the young in the Beat Generation, so as this book comes back onto bookshelves it will have—in your hands, reader—a different life.

* * *

Change was something that Bashō understood. He was born in Ueno, near Kyoto, in 1644, not long after the death of Shakespeare in the last days of medieval Japan. His father, a gentleman farmer of the samurai class, died when Bashō was eleven. He went into the service of his feudal lord, whose son Yoshitada became his close friend and introduced him to the world of poetry. When he was twenty-two, his friend died suddenly, and Bashō found his way to the capitol city of Edo. There he quickly became an admired writer of *haikai*, or linked verses, and it was not long before he was an established master-teacher. His students built him a hut on the edge of town and called it the Bashō hut, for the great floppy leaved banana tree, or *bashō*, that dominated the garden. After the two immense losses of his early years, he had made a life. Then, in 1683, in a fire that destroyed much of Edo, the Bashō hut burned down. Although his students wanted to rebuild it, Bashō chose not to return to a settled life and instead took to the road.

He wrote a poem about it, evoking all of his favorite travelers and spiritual wanderers—Kerouac's bhikku—in the Chinese and Japanese tradition. It goes like this in my translation:

> Su Tung-p'o, slanting his traveler's hat would look up toward the cloudy sky, and Tu Fu, wearing a hat heavy with snow, would roam faraway places. Since I have plenty of time here at this grassy hut, I have made a rainproof hat with my own hands in imitation of the hat Saigyō wore in his solitary wanderings:

Life in this world—
a makeshift hut
like Sōgi's

He set out on his travels in 1684 and recorded them in a series of five poetic diaries. The last and longest of them, *Oku-no-hosomichi*, is based on a nine-month, fifteen-hundred-mile trek through the rugged mountainous north of Japan. *Recorded* is probably not the right word. While the first of the diaries, *Journal of a Weathered Skeleton*, is probably just that, jottings, poems and scraps of prose impressions composed on the road, in these last years of his life Bashō refined and shaped the form. How much he did so scholars can in this case tell, because Bashō's companion Sora kept a more workman-like account of their trip.

In Bashō's time there was, already, a long Japanese tradition of pilgrimage, not only to religious but also to historical shrines, since

Japanese culture had made a kind of religion of its history. And if you begin by thinking of this book as something like a late medieval European pilgrim's account of his travels and the religious emotions it gave rise to (in a way that is what *Don Quixote* is), you will get the spirit of it. Or, better yet, think of it as an example of a book at the tail end of that tradition turning itself into one of the first modern works of art.

Working on the earlier journals and on the headnotes to his poems, Bashō developed a haiku-like prose style that came to be called *haibun*. It was rapid, allusive, suggestive, and aimed at something like the aesthetic ideal of *yūgen*. In *Okyu-no-hosomichi* he brought it to its highest development. In his study of Bashō, Makoto Ueda remarks that one way of thinking about the book is to see it as fifty or so *haibun*, prose poems that end with a final leap to haiku. Ueda also observes that as Bashō travels from shrine to shrine through the back country he travels through time as well as space. It's easy to see how both of these things are true of the passage I quoted earlier. Bashō has come to Ryushakuji, to a temple founded by Jikaku Daishi, an important Japanese teacher of Buddhism who had, eight hundred years earlier, in the days of Han Shan, traveled to T'ang dynasty China to study there and left behind a pilgrim's journal. Bashō gives a quick, seemingly casual but almost allegorical account of his arrival at a place where, as Kerouac's Ray Smith says, someone had turned the wheel of the dharma. First the worldly setting, then the ascent, and in three swift phrases the experience of the meaning of the place, "penetrating scene, profound quietness, heart/mind clear." And then the small poem of the powerful inward drive of the experience—the sound of the cicada in the stillness seeming almost to drill itself into the rock.

*Oku-no-hosomichi* is full of such moments, and in *Back Roads to Far Towns* they come alive in English. It's a good thing to have back in print a great book in an inspired translation.

# INTRODUCTION

EARLY ONE SPRING MORNING IN 1689 BASHŌ AC-
companied by his friend and disciple Sora set forth from Edo (old Tokyo)
on the long nine-month journey which was to take them through the
backlands and highlands north of the capital and then west to the Japan
Sea coast and along it until they turned inland again towards Lake Biwa
(near Kyoto). Approximately the first half of this journey, the most ar-
duous part, remains recorded in the *Oku-no-hosomichi*.

Bashō in his 46th year and Sora in his 41st had lived quietly near each
other for some time. The journey was one both had looked forward to and
realized would be difficult and even dangerous. And, indeed, one might
*not* return. It was to be more a pilgrimage—and in the garb of pilgrims
they went—than a case of wandering scholarship: a sight not uncommon
even in modern Japan, visiting from temple to temple, seeing old acquaintances, places famed in history or poetry or legend, touchstones for
the life lived, the dying to come and what life continues.

By then Bashō had already earned a far-flung reputation as a *haikai*
poet and master and was much awaited and sought out: he was himself
invariably the occasion *for* poetry.

Most of his poetry (and it is within the tradition which he himself was
shaping) evokes a context and wants one. The poems are not isolated

7

instances of lyricism, but cries of their occasions, of some one intently passing through a world, often arrested by the momentary nature of things within an unfathomable "order."

If, at times, the poems seem slight, remember that mere profusion, words piled up "about" event, often give an illusion of importance and scale belied by the modest proportions of human destiny. Precise conjunction of language and feeling, appropriately sounded, directness and fulness in brevity, residual aptness and alertness, mark *haiku* at best (as in those of Bashō): grounded in season and particularity, no matter how allusive. "Down-to-earth and firm-grained."

Sora also kept a journal of this trip, but it remains as a strictly factual "check"—while Bashō made his into (essentially) a poem (after some years) that has become a center of the Japanese mind/heart.

We too move out with him to and through the backwater regions of north central Honshū. His words are our provision, breath, rhythm. And they can never not be our time. The end of his journey is the end of ours. Everywhere he goes one feels a sounding made, the ground hallowed, hardwon, endeared to him, and so to us, through what others had made of it, had reached, discovered.

So many today who have lost touch have lost touch with just such grounds for being.

When tears come to Bashō it may seem that he is merely being soppy (one might say the same of Dante or of Stendhal, though both are also "tough"). A man's sentiments, however, are not disputable. But if we feel what it is to live and to be dying, each one alone, know what cherishing is and *see* what Bashō sees into tears, we may realize that there is a sympathy that enlarges the spirit without destroying it that obtains for man a more complete sense of relation to his world.

What Bashō doesnt say moves at least as much as what he does. One knows his silences go deeper than reasons. And when his eyes plumb words for heart—when the heart holds the island of Sado, locus of exile, at the crest of a brimming sea, and the eye lifts from that pointed violence and loneliness on the horizon to the stars flowing effortlessly up and over and back into the man making vision, who has not at once felt all language vanish into a wholeness and scope of sense that lifts one as if one weighed nothing?

8

*Bashō*

Whether, when we go to him, return to him, as many of us must when we are most alone, we feel much as he does in his last entry, elated, back with old friends, or not, remains for each to find out. But the hope is in bringing this text over into English that some will open wider for it, discover the heart's, spirit's, geography refreshed—"read" (as a Noh teacher said apropos of reading a Noh text) as one who has travelled and climbed and come down and who knows he has still harder going ahead "reads" a map.

Meanwhile a summer's journey awaits, two men are about to depart on foot, one of them already thinks of us.

10

# TRANSLATORS' PREFACE

MORE AND MORE WE LIVE AT A TIME WHEN THE foreign is no longer exotic, when romantic images of past ages no longer either convince or suffice. And with this changing attitude perhaps a more salutary, more perceptive, sense of what experiences the past offered and still offers can be brought to bear in such translations as the one now before you.

If the translators have often not accepted Western approximations for particular Japanese and/or Chinese terms, it is not to create undue difficulties for readers, but rather to admit an exactitude otherwise impossible. As a result, notes may be needed in greater profusion than before.

Bashō's "style" is a *haiku*-style: terse and to the point, while being allusive to the degree of T'ang poetry. We have tried to maintain the feel of his sometimes unusual syntax, the flow and economy of his language. The poems should help *clot* passages, so that one doesnt read too rapidly, and the brief marginal notations may also help break (brake) pace.

The Japanese text is based on the best available versions and the most authoritative Japanese scholarship; variant readings are included in parentheses.

The illustrations are by Hayakawa Ikutada, a contemporary *haiga* painter, and appear here through the courtesy of the artist and the Yamada Art Gallery, Kyoto.

A map of Bashō's journey is included after the notes.

11

# PRONUNCIATION GUIDE

AS MANY READERS WILL BY NOW KNOW, IN READING Romanized equivalents of Japanese words (and consonants are not breathed and shaped in quite the same way), each syllable wants virtually equal stress and clarity—though the vowel "u" tends at times, especially in final position, to be slurred—at least in our time. The vowels are much like those in Italian and invariable.

"a" sounds like "*ah*," "e" as in "*fey*;" *Date*, for example, is pronounced: Dah-tay. The "i" sounds as in "*machine*;" "o" as in "*or*;" "u" as in "*rule*." Long marks mean longer soundings: quantitatively and by transfer create a sense of accent.

12

# BACK ROADS TO FAR TOWNS

月日は百代の過客にして、行かふ年も又旅人也。舟の上に生涯をうかべ、馬の口とらえて老をむかふる物は、日々旅にして旅を栖とす。古人も多く旅に死せるあり。予もいづれの年よりか、片雲の風にさそはれて、漂泊の思ひやまず、海濱にさすらへ、去年の秋、江上の破屋に蜘の古巣をはらひて、やゝ年も暮、春立る霞の空に白川の関こえんと、そゞろ神の物につきて心をくるはせ、道祖神のまねきにあひて取もの手につかず、もゝ引の破をつゞり笠の緒付かえて、三里に灸すゆるより、松嶋の月先心にかゝりて、住る方は人に譲り杉風が別墅に移るに、

　　　　　草の戸も住替る代ぞひなの家

面八句を庵の柱に懸置。

14

## 1

MOON & SUN ARE PASSING FIGURES OF
countless generations, and years coming or going wanderers too.
Drifting life away on a boat or meeting age leading a horse by
the mouth, each day is a journey and the journey itself home.
Amongst those of old were many that perished upon the journey.
So—when was it—I, drawn like blown cloud, couldnt stop
dreaming of roaming, roving the coast up and down, back at
the hut last fall by the river side, sweeping cobwebs off, a year
gone and misty skies of spring returning, yearning to go over the
Shirakawa Barrier, possessed by the wanderlust, at wits' end,
beckoned by Dōsojin, hardly able to keep my hand to any thing,
mending a rip in my *momohiki*, replacing the cords in my *kasa*,
shins no sooner burnt with moxa than the moon at Matsushima
rose to mind and how, my former dwelling passed on to someone
else on moving to Sampū's summer house,

*(1689)*

momohiki: *light
cotton britches*
kasa: *peaked sedge or
bamboo rain & sun
hat*

> the grass door too
> turning into
> a dolls' house

(from the eight *omote*) set on a post of the hut.

15

*departing spring (ya . . .*

弥生も末の七日、明ぼのゝ空朧々として、月は在明にて光おさまれる物から、不二の峯幽にみえて、上野谷中の花の梢又いつかはと心ぼそし。むつましきかぎりは宵よりつどひて、舟に乗て送る。千じゆと云所にて船をあがれば、前途三千里のおもひ胸にふさがりて、幻のちまたに離別の泪をそゝく。

行春や鳥啼魚の目は泪

是を矢立の初として、行道なをすゝまず。人々は途中に立ならびて、後かげのみゆる迄はと見送なるべし。

18

## 2

YAYOI: LAST SEVENTH, SLIGHTLY HAZY
dawn, "a waning moon, a failing light," summit of Fuji vague,
crowns of blossoming cherry at Ueno and Yanaka, when would
they—and would they—be seen again? Friends, gathering since
nightfall, came along by boat to see us off. Landed at Senju,
sense of three thousand *li* ahead swelling the heart, world so
much a dream, tears at point of departure.

li: *Chinese measure, sim. to Eng. league, about 2.5 mi.*

> departing spring (ya
> birds cry fishes'
> eyes tears

the *yatate*'s first words, the path
taken looked not to advance at all. Those filling the way behind
watched till only shadows of backs seemed seen.

yatate: *portable brush & sumi ink kit*

19

　　　　　ことし元禄二とせにや、奥羽長途の行脚只かりそめに思ひたち
て、呉天に白髪の恨を重ぬといへ共、耳にふれていまだめに見ぬさかひ、若生て歸らばと定
なき賴の末をかけ、其日漸早加と云宿にたどり着にけり。痩骨の肩にかゝれる物先くるし
む。只身すがらにと出立侍を、帋子一衣は夜の防ぎ、ゆかた・雨具・墨筆のたぐひ、あるは
さりがたき餞などしたるは、さすがに打捨がたくて路次の煩となれるこそわりなけれ。

3

Ōü: *variant of Oku*

kamiko: *strong paper clothing*
yukata: *light summer clothing*
hanamuke: *farewell gifts*

THIS YEAR, THE SECOND—IS IT—OF THE Genroku, far only to think how far it is to Ōu "under Go skies," to picture hair turning white, places ears had heard of eyes never seen, likelihood of returning not so bright, just did make the post town of Sōka by nightfall. Thin shoulders feeling packs drag. Body enough, but burdened with a set of *kamiko* (extra protection at night), *yukata*, raincoat, ink-stick, brushes, as well as unavoidable *hanamuke*, etc., somehow hard to let go of, part of the trouble in travelling inevitably.

室の八嶋に詣す。同行曽良が曰、「此神は木の花さくや姫の神と申て冨士一躰也。無戸室に入て焼給ふちかひのみ中に、火々出見のみこと生れ給ひしより室の八嶋と申。又煙を讀習し侍もこの謂也。」將このしろといふ魚を禁ず縁記の旨世に伝ふ事も侍し。

22

## 4

VISITED THE MURO-NO-YASHIMA. MY companion, Sora, said: "The deity here, Konohana Sakuya Hime, is the same as that at Fuji. She went and set fire to the Utsu-muro to prove her innocence and out of this was Prince Hohodemi born and the place called Muro-no-Yashima. And why poetry written about it mentions smoke." Also fish known as *konoshiro* prohibited here. Story behind it common knowledge.

23

*O glorious/green leaves . . .*

卅日、日光山の麓に泊る。あるじの云けるやう、「我名を佛五左衛門と云。萬正直を旨とする故に、人かくは申侍まゝ、一夜の草の枕も打解て休み給へ」と云。いかなる仏の濁世塵土に示現して、かゝる桑門の乞食順礼ごときの人をたすけ給ふにやと、あるじのなす事に心をとゞめてみるに、唯無智無分別にして正直偏固の者也。剛毅木訥の仁に近きたぐひ、氣稟の清質 尤 尊ぶべし。

26

5

(*March 30, act. Apr 1*)
Nikkō: *lit. "sun
 light"*
Hotoke Gozaemon:
 *like saying—Jack
 Buddha*

THIRTIETH. STAYED AT FOOT OF MT.
Nikkō. Hosteler says: "They call me Hotoke Gozaemon. Ho-
nesty's a habit with me, which is why the name, so feel right to
home," what he said. Impossible not to realize how Buddha
appears upon this mean and muddled ground in just such guise
to help shaman beggar pilgrims on, seeing our host's simple
sincere manner, frank and down-to-earth. Firm-grained and
unassuming, the very image of the man of *jen*, worthy of all
respect.

卯月朔日、御山に詣拝す。往昔此御山を二荒山と書しを、空海大師開基の時日光と改給ふ。千歳未來をさとり給ふにや、今此御光一天にかゝやきて，恩沢八荒にあふれ、四民安堵の栖穏なり。猶憚多くて筆をさし置ぬ。

あらたうと青葉若葉の日の光

28

## 6

(*Apr 1st*)
Uzuki: *lit. "month of
the U flower"*
Futarayama: *lit.
"Two Wastes Mt"*
*(also read Nikōzan)*

eight directions:
*8 major compass
points*

FIRST OF UZUKI, CALLED ON THE mountain shrine. Originally this mountain known as Futarayama, but when Kūkai Daishi dedicated the shrine here, he renamed it Nikkō. Perhaps with presentiment those thousand years ago of the splendor now gracing our skies and the blessings extended to the eight directions to the four classes of citizens living in peace. But with glory so full, so empty are words.

> O glorious
> green leaves young leaves'
> sun light

黒髪山（くろかみやま）は霞かゝりて、雪いまだ白し。

剃捨（そりすて）て黒髪山に衣更（ころもがへ）　　　曽良

曽良は河合氏（かはひうぢ）にして、惣五郎（そうごらう）と云へり。芭蕉の下葉（したば）に軒をならべて、予が薪水（しんすゐ）の労をたすく。このたび松しま・象潟（きさかた）の眺（ながめ）共にせん事を悦び、且は羈旅（きりよ）の難をいたはらんと、旅立暁（たびだつあかつき）髪を剃（そり）て墨染（すみぞめ）にさまをかえ、惣五を改（あらため）て宗悟（そうご）とす。仍（よつ）て墨（黒）髪山の句有（あり）。衣更の二字力ありてきこゆ。

廿餘丁（にじふよちやう）山を登つて瀧有（あり）。岩洞（がんとう）の頂（いただき）より飛流して百尺、千岩の碧潭（へきたん）に落（おち）たり。岩窟（がんくつ）に身をひそめ入（いり）て滝の裏（うしろ）よりみれば、うらみ（裏見）の瀧（まうしつた）と申伝え侍る也。

暫時（しばらく）は瀧に籠（こも）るや夏の初（はじめ）

30

## 7

(*Apr 2*)
Kurokami: *lit.*
  *"Black Hair"*

still snow clad.

> head shaven
> at Mt Kurokami
> changing apparel
>
>             (Sora)

bashō: *the plantain*
  *tree*

Sora formerly Kawai Sōgorō. In *bashō* shade, eave to eave, helped at wood and water chores. Delighted at the chance to share prospects of Matsushima and Kisakata, offered to take on whatever tasks the journey would call for, at dawn of the day of departure had head shaven, assumed pilgrim garb and signalled the new life by changing name to Sōgo. And so, the Mt Kurokami poem. The words "changing apparel" weigh tellingly.

chō: *about 120 yards*
shaku: *almost precisely our "foot"*
Urami: *lit.*
  *"Back View"*

Climbed more than twenty *chō* uphill to find the waterfall. Plunges from over cavern a hundred *shaku* down to thousand-rock-studded basin below. Stooped into cavern to peer out from behind cascade known as Urami Falls.

> for a while
> to a waterfall confined
> summer opening

31

*for a while/to a waterfall . . .*

　　　　　那須の黒ばねと云所に知人あれば、是より野越にかゝりて直道
をゆかんとす。遙に一村を見かけて行に雨降日暮る。農夫の家に一夜をかりて、明れば又野中
を行。そこに野飼の馬あり。草刈おのこになげきよれば、野夫といへどもさすがに情しらぬ
には非ず、「いかゞすべきや、されども此野は縦横にわかれて、うゐうゐ敷旅人の道ふみた
がえん、あやしう侍れば、此馬のとゞまる所にて馬を返し給へ」とかし侍ぬ。ちいさき者ふ
たり馬の跡したひてはしる。独は小姫にて名をかさねと云。聞なれぬ名のやさしかりければ、

　　　　　かさねとは八重撫子の名成べし　　　曽良

頓て人里に至れば、あたひを鞍つぼに結付て馬を返しぬ。

## 8

(*Apr 3*)

SET OUT FOR PLACE CALLED KURO-
bane in Nasu to see an acquaintance there and tried shortcut
through fields. Caught sight of a village not too far off, made
for it, rain starting, evening coming on. Passed night at a
farmhouse and next morning tried crossing fields again.
Horse pastured there. Asked the way of a fellow mowing nearby
who, plain as he was, wasnt without courtesy. "Let me see,"
he says, "you know this here field cuts off different ways and if
you dont know which is which, worse luck, easy to get lost, so
better let the horse there take you far as he can and when he
stops, just send him back," and he lent us the horse.

Two tiny creatures scampered behind. One a darling called
Kasane. A curious sweet name:

> this *kasane*
> pretty double pink's
> name naturally
> (Sora)

Soon at the village, tied something for owner to saddle and
sent horse back.

35

黒羽の舘代浄坊寺何がしの方に音信る。思ひがけぬあるじの悦
び、日夜語つゞけて、其弟桃翠など云が朝夕勤とぶらひ、自の家にも伴ひて、親属の方にも
まねかれ日をふるまゝに、ひとひ郊外に逍遥して犬追物の跡を一見し、那須の篠原をわけて
玉藻の前の古墳をとふ。それより八幡宮に詣。与市扇の的を射し時、別しては我國氏神正八
まんとちかひしも、此神社にて侍と聞ば、感應殊しきりに覺えらる。暮れば桃翠宅に歸る。
　　修驗光明寺と云有。そこにまねかれて行者堂を拜す。

　　　　夏 山 に 足 駄 を 拜 む 首 途 哉

36

## 9

VISITED A CERTAIN JŌBŌJI, KANDAI OF Kurobane. With unanticipated pleasure talked day and night, his brother Tōsui coming over faithfully morning and evening had us to his place and then, at their instance, to relatives of his, and days passed: one in strolling about the outskirts, inspecting the site of the *Inuoümono*, another in wandering around the Nasu reed-brakes to see Tamamo-no-mae's old tomb. Then praying at the Hachiman shrine. When Yoichi aimed at and struck the fan down, the prayer he uttered was: "Above all, to Shō-hachiman, god of my nativeland," referring to this shrine, and the grace of that response realized touches deep. At nightfall returned to Tōsui's.

*gyōjadō: hall for* yamabushi *priest austerities*

Temple there called Shugen-kōmyōji. Invited, visited its *gyōjadō*.

> summer mountains
> praying to *ashida*
> for a start

當國雲岸寺のおくに佛頂和尚山居跡あり。

　「竪横の五尺にたらぬ草の庵

　むすぶもくやし雨なかりせば

と松の炭して岩に書付侍り」と、いつぞや聞え給ふ。其跡みんと雲岸寺に杖を曳ば、人々すすんで共にいざなひ、若き人おほく道のほど打さはぎて、おぼえず彼梺に到る。山はおくあるけしきにて、谷道遙に松杉黑く苔したゞりて、卯月の天今猶寒し。十景盡る所、橋をわたつて山門に入。

　さて、かの跡はいづくのほどにやと、後の山によぢのぼれば、石上の小庵岩窟にむすびかけたり。妙禪師の死関、法雲法師の石室をみるがごとし。

　　木啄も庵はやぶらず夏木立

と、とりあへぬ一句を柱に殘侍し。

38

## 10

BURIED IN THE VICINITY OF UN-
ganji the spot Butchō-oshō lived in mountain retreat.

> less than five-foot square
> thatched abode

> a pity to put up at all
> but there *is* rain

(*Apr 5*)

                                                                   :what he wrote with pine-charcoal point on rock—how long ago was that told? To see what remains led our walking-sticks to Unganji and some kindly beckoning others to come along too, mostly younger people, got caught up in such eager chatter, reached mountain unawares. Dense, a long way through the valley, pine and cedar thick massed, moss oozing, *Uzuki* sky chilly. Where the ten views ended, crossed a bridge and entered by temple gate.

    Then, intent on our quest, scrambled up just beyond and there it was, the hut, perched on a ledge up against a cave. Like seeing Myōzenji's "Entrance to Death" or Hōun-Hōshi's "Stone Chamber."

> even woodpeckers
> can't break into this hut
> summer grove

                                    hastily written, the one poem, left on a post there.

是より殺生石に行。舘代より馬にて送らる。此口付のおのこ、「短冊得させよ」と乞。やさしき事を望侍るものかなと、

　　　野を横に馬牽むけよほとゝぎす

殺生石は温泉の出る山陰にあり。石の毒氣いまだほろびず、蜂・蝶のたぐひ眞砂の色の見えぬほどかさなり死す。

## 11

AFTERWARDS OFF TO THE SESSHŌSEKI
on horse sent by the *kandai*. Man leading it by halter asked
for a *tanzaku*. Beautiful he wanted one:

tanzaku: *narrow
    strip of fine paper
    to write poetry on;
    i.e., a poem*
hototogisu: *Japanese
    cuckoo, whose name
    is its song*

> across the fields
> head the horse
> *hototogisu*

The Sesshōseki in mountain shadow where hot springs flow.
Noxious fumes of the rock not yet abated and such a pile of
dead butterflies bees and other bugs sand underneath hard
to see.

又、清水ながるゝの柳は蘆野の里にありて田の畔に残る。此所の郡守戸部某の、此柳みせばやなど折々にの給ひ聞え給ふを、いづくのほどにやと思ひしを、今日此柳のかげにこそ立より侍つれ。

田一枚植て立去る柳かな

## 12

(Apr 20)

gunshu: *feudal deputy governor*

YES, AT ASHINO THERE'S STILL THE willow of the "pacing stream" on a path amid fields. A certain Kobu, *gunshu* of the region, had often offered to show us the tree and had wondered exactly where it was and today at last in that very willow's shade.

a patch of rice
planting done leaving
the willow there

43

心許なき日かず重るまゝに、白川の関にかゝりて旅心定りぬ。いかで都へと便求しも断也。中にも此関は三関の一にして、風騒の人心をとゞむ。秋風を耳に殘し、紅葉も俤にして、青葉の梢猶あはれ也。卯の花の白妙に、茨の花の咲そひて、雪にもこゆる心地ぞする。古人冠を正し衣裝を改し事など、清輔の筆にもとゞめ置れしとぞ。

　　　卯の花をかざしに関の晴着かな　　　曾良

44

## 13

(*Apr 21*)

Miyako: *the "capital," usually Kyoto in old poetry; here B wd. mean Edo*

unohana: (Deutzia scabra) *small white flowers*

kanmuri: *small black formal hat, held in place by a pin*

towards the Shirakawa Barrier, but mind each day calmer clearer for continuing. Of course felt like "somehow sending word to Miyako." After all, one of the Three Barriers, and others of poetic bent left word of feeling behind. "Autumnal winds" hummed in my ears, "the maple" stood imagined, but leafgreen branches haunting too. Against *unohana* white white briars, as if pushing through snow. Here, according to Kiyosuke's brush, long ago a man put on the *kanmuri* and donned courtly costume.

> *unohana*
> adorning the head
> barrier regalia
>
> (Sora)

45

とかくして越行まゝに、あぶくま川を渡る。左に会津根高く、右に岩城・相馬・三春の庄、常陸・下野の地をさかひて山つらなる。かげ沼と云所を行に、今日は空曇て物影うつらず。

　すか川の驛に等窮といふものを尋て、四五日とゞめらる。先「白河の関いかにこえつるや」と問。「長途のくるしみ、身心つかれ、且は風景に魂うばゝれ、懐旧に腸を断て、はかばかしう思ひめぐらさず。

　　　　　風流の初やおくの田植うた

無下にこえんもさすがに」と語れば、脇・第三とつゞけて、三巻となしぬ。

## 14

SO WE WENT OVER AND CROSSED THE
Abukumagawa. To left, high summits of Aizu, and to right,
the demesnes of Iwaki, Sōma and Miharu, divided by mountain ranges from Hitachi and Shimotsuke. Passed place called
Kagenuma, but overcast sky hindered reflection.

Kagenuma: *Shadow
Pond, or Mirror
Pond*
(*Apr 22*)

At post town of Sukagawa visited one Tōkyū and were
had to stay four or five days. First thing he did was ask: "Anything come of crossing the Shirakawa Barrier?" "What with
the aches of so much travelling, with body and mind exhausted,
apart from being entranced simply by the scene and remember-
ing other times, there wasnt much chance for thinking words
of my own through.

> *fūryū's*
> beginning Oku's
> rice-planting song

all that the crossing brought," my reply, which, emended by
a *waki* and *daisan*, led to composing three sequences.

*this* kasane . . .

此宿の傍に、大きなる栗の木陰をたのみて、世をいとふ僧有。橡ひろふ太山もかくやと聞に覺られて、ものに書付侍る。其詞、

栗といふ文字は西の木と書て、西方淨土に便ありと、行基菩薩の一生杖にも柱にも此木を用給ふとかや、

世の人の見付ぬ花や軒の栗

15

OFF ON THE EDGE OF TOWN, IN THE
shade of a huge chestnut tree, a priest, completely out of things.
Perhaps "in mountain depths gathering chestnuts" referred to
such an existence, or so to my imagination it seemed and, given
something to write on, wrote: "literally *kanji* for 'chestnut'
(栗) read 'west tree,' they say alludes to the Western Paradise,
and Gyōgi Bosatsu, they say, during his lifetime used it for his
walking-stick and the posts of his house."

kanji: *Chinese ideogram*

most folks'
unseen flowers
the eaves' chestnut

　　　　　　等窮が宅を出て五里計、檜皮の宿を離れてあさか山有。路より近し。此あたり沼多し。かつみ刈比もやゝ近うなれば、「いづれの草を花かつみとは云ぞ」と、人々に尋侍れども、更知人なし。沼を尋、人にとひ、かつみかつみと尋ありきて、日は山の端にかゝりぬ。二本松より右にきれて、黒塚の岩屋一見し、福嶋に宿る。

## 16

(*May 1st*)

FROM TŌKYŪ'S PLACE ABOUT FIVE *li* to post town of Hihada, and Mt Asaka just beyond. Off the road a ways. Mostly marshland hereabouts. *Katsumi*-gathering time near, asking people about the so-called *hana-katsumi*, but none knew. Poking about the marshes, asking everyone met, roaming around in search of *katsumi katsumi*, sun grazing mountain ridge. Turned right at Nihonmatsu and looked into Kurozuka cavern and stayed over in Fukushima.

あくれば、しのぶもぢ摺の石を尋て忍ぶのさとに行。遙山陰の小里に、石半土に埋てあり。里の童部の来りて教ける、「昔は此山の上に侍しを、往來の人の麦草をあらして此石を試侍をにくみて、此谷につき落せば、石の面下ざまにふしたり」と云。さもあるべき事にや。

　　　早苗とる手もとや昔しのぶ摺

54

## 17

NEXT DAY, WENT AROUND ASKING
for *Shinobu-mojizuri* rock, reaching Shinobu village. At a
hamlet just the other side of the mountain the rock, half-
buried in earth. Some village children tagged along and explained. In olden times, they said, it used to be up on top of the
mountain, but villagers tired of people passing through tearing
out their green grain to try on rock bowled it over into valley
so face now hidden. Might well have been so.

seedlings pluck
handroot old
*Shinobuzuri*

55

fūryū's/*beginning* . . .

月の輪のわたしを越て、瀬の上と云宿に出づ。佐藤庄司が旧跡は左の山際一里半計に有。飯塚の里、鯖野と聞て、尋々行に、丸山と云に尋あたる。是庄司が旧舘也。梺に大手の跡など人の敎ゆるにまかせて泪を落し、又かたはらの古寺に一家の石碑を残す。中にも二人の嫁がしるし先哀也。女なれどもかひがひしき名の世に聞えつる物かなと袂をぬらしぬ。堕涙の石碑も遠きにあらず。寺に入て茶を乞へば、爰に義經の太刀・弁慶が笈をとゞめて什物とす。

　　　　笠 も 太 刀 も 五 月 に か ざ れ 帋 幟

五月朔日の事也。

58

18

TOOK FERRY AT TSUKINOWA, TO
post town of Se-no-ue. Site of Satō Shōji's to be found to the
left about *li* and a half away. Heard it was at Sabano in
Iizuka and kept enquiring on the way, finally locating
mountain called Maruyama. Here remains of his castle are.
At bottom, ruins of main gate, etc., and seeing them so, eyes
fill, and at old temple hard-by, family graves. Tombs of
young wives of two sons most felt. The story of their heroism,
though women, has come down, sleeve at my eyes. The
Weeping Rock can't be very different. Went into temple for
tea, where Yoshitsune's long-sword and Benkei's *oi* are kept
as treasures.

oi: *wickerwork chest for Buddhist gear (May 1st, but actually 2nd)*

> chest too and sword
> in May hoist high as
> paper standards

Satsuki: *old calendar, May: "rice-planting month"*

This occurred on the first of *Satsuki.*

59

其夜飯塚にとまる。温泉あれば湯に入て宿をかるに、土坐に莚を敷てあやしき貧家也。灯もなければゐろりの火かげに寝所をまうけて臥す。夜に入て雷鳴、雨しきりに降て、臥る上よりもり、蚤蚊にせゝられて眠らず。持病さへおこりて消入計になん。短夜の空もやうやう明れば、又旅立ぬ。猶夜の余波心すゝまず、馬かりて桑折の驛に出る。遙なる行末をかゝえて、斯る病覚束なしといへど、羇旅邊土の行脚、捨身無常の觀念、道路にしなん、是天の命なりと、氣力聊とり直し、路縦横に踏で伊達の大木戸をこす。

## 19

SPENT NIGHT AT IIZUKA. BATHED AT hot-springs there, found lodgings but only thin mats over bare earth, ramshackle sort of place. No lamp, bedded down by shadowy light of fireplace and tried getting some rest. All night, thunder, pouring buckets, roof leaking, fleas mosquitoes in droves: no sleep. To cap it off the usual trouble cropped up, almost passed out. The short night sky at last broke, and again picked up and went on. But the night's traces dragged, mind balked. Hired horses, got to post town of Ko-ori. Future seemed further off than ever, and recurring illness nagged, but what a pilgrimage to far places calls for: willingness to let world go, its momentariness, to die on the road, human destiny, which lifted spirit a little, finding foot again here and there, crossing the Ōkido Barrier in Date.

鐙摺・白石の城を過、笠嶋の郡に入れば、藤中將実方の塚はいづくのほどならんと人にとへば、「是より遙右に見ゆる山際の里をみのわ・笠嶋と云、道祖神の社、かた見の薄今にあり」と教ゆ。此比の五月雨に道いとあしく、身つかれ侍れば、よそながら眺やりて過るに、簑輪・笠嶋も五月雨の折にふれたりと、

　　　笠嶋はいづこさ月のぬかり道

岩沼に宿る。

62

20

AFTER PASSING ABUMIZURI AND
Shiroishi Castle, entered the district of Kasashima, and sought
out Tō-no-chūjō Sanekata's grave: far to right among slopes
could be seen villages of Minowa and Kasashima, where
Dōsojin shrine and *susuki* grass of memory remain. What with
May rains the road impossible and, much too tired, gazed at
them from afar, Minowa and Kasashima—apt for the season,

*(May 4)*
susuki: *sedge*
Minowa: *"Straw raincoat"*
Kasashima: *"Umbrella Isle"*

> Kasashima's
> where on May's
> mud-ridden road

and put up at Iwanuma.

63

武隈の松にこそめ覚る心地はすれ。根は土際より二木にわかれて、昔の姿うしなはずとしらる。先能因法師思ひ出。往昔むつのかみにて下りし人、此木を伐て名取川の橋杭にせられたる事などあればにや、「松は此たび跡もなし」とは詠たり。代々あるは伐、あるひは植継などせしと聞に、今將千歳のかたちとゝのほひて、めでたき松のけしきになん侍し。

「武隈の松みせ申せ遅桜」

と挙白と芸ものゝ餞別したりければ、

桜より松は二木を三月越シ

64

## 21

At its roots trunk breaks into two arms, probably much as in olden times, nothing lost. Immediately Nōin-Hōshi came to mind. Before his time the Lord of Mutsu had come and had the tree cut down to help provide lumber for bridge over the Natorigawa, which may account for his writing: "no sign there now of the pine." Time and time again, said to have been replaced, cut down, and now standing, the image of a thousand years in fine shape again, miraculous.

> offer him
> Takekuma's pine
> O late-blossoming cherry

given me on departing by one known as Kyohaku, now elicits:

> since cherry blossoms
> yearning for the two trunked pine
> three months after.

65

名取川を渡て仙臺に入。あやめふく日也。旅宿をもとめて四五日逗留す。爰に畫工加右衞門と云ものあり。聊心ある者と聞て知る人になる。この者、「年比さだかならぬ名どころを考置侍れば」とて、一日案内す。宮城野の萩茂りあひて、秋の氣色思ひやらるゝ。玉田・よこ野、つゝじが岡はあせび咲ころ也。日影ももらぬ松の林に入て、爰を木の下と云とぞ。昔もかく露ふかければこそ、「みさぶらひみかさ」とはよみたれ。薬師堂・天神の御社など拝て、其日はくれぬ。猶、松嶋・塩がまの所々畫に書て送る。且、紺の染緒つけたる草鞋二足餞す。さればこそ風流のしれもの、爰に至りて其實を顯す。

　　　あやめ艸足に結ん草鞋の緒

66

## 22

*(May 7)*

hagi: *bush clover,*
  *tiny pink or white*
  *blossoms*
Tsutsuji-ga-oka:
  *Azalea Hill*
asebi: *small white*
  *bell-shaped clusters*
Konoshita:
  *"Under Woods"*

Sendai. Day of plaiting eaves with blue flags. Found an inn and stayed four or five days. Painter here called Kaemon. Had heard of him as one of not a little spirit and met. For many years he'd hunted up places once famous in the area but now obscure and one day showed us around. *Hagi* so thick in Miyagi Fields, could sense what fall must be like. Tamada, Yokono, and at Tsutsuji-ga-oka *asebi* flowers near peak bloom. Went through pine woods so dense sun can't penetrate, place called Konoshita. Once long ago the heavy dewfall led to, "Attendants, an umbrella" 's being written here. Visited the Yakushi-dō and Tenjin Shrine, and some other places as sun descended. And he showed and gave us sketches of parts of Matsushima and Shiogama. And added two pairs of straw sandals, cords dyed dark-blue, as *hanamuke*. So, indeed, was he seen as one of true *fūryū*.

> ah to have blue flags
> bound to one's feet
> straw sandal cords

67

　　　　　　　かの畫圖にまかせてたどり行ば、おくの細道の山際に十符の菅
有。今も年々十符の菅菰を調て國守に献ずと云り。

## 壺碑　市川村多賀城に有

　つぼの石ぶみは、高サ六尺餘、横三尺計歟。苔を穿て文字幽也。四維國界之数里をし
るす。「此城、神亀元年、按察使鎮守符將軍大野朝臣東人之所置也。天平宝字六年、參議
東海東山節度使、同將軍恵美朝臣獦修造而、十二月朔日」と有。聖武皇帝の御時に
當れり。むかしよりよみ置る歌枕、おほく語傳ふといへども、山崩川流て道あらたまり、
石は埋て土にかくれ、木は老て若木にかはれば、時移り代變じて、其跡たしかならぬ事の
みを、爰に至りて疑なき千歳の記念、今眼前に古人の心を閲す。行脚の一徳、存命の悦び、
羇旅の勞をわすれて泪も落るばかり也。

68

## 23

went, skirting mountains; alongside winding Oku-no-hosomi-chi Tofu sedge. People here still make annual tribute of ten-stitch sedge mats to the *kokushu*.

kokushu: *prefectural governor*

The Tsubo-no-ishibumi found at Taga Castle in village of Ichikawa. More than six *shaku* high and maybe three *shaku* wide. Words vaguely made out through moss. Distances in *li* to the frontier at all four cross-points marked. Castle originally erected in first year of Jinki by Ōno-no-ason Azumabito, *azechi* and *chinjufu shōgun*. In sixth year of Tempyō-hōji, Emi-no-ason Asakari, *sangi* and *setsudoshi* for Tōkai and Tōzan, had it repaired. On first day of the twelfth moon, it records. Time of Emperor Shōmu. Many old places brought down to us through poetry, but landslides and floods have altered paths and covered markers with earth, and trees arisen generations gone, and hard to locate anything now, but that moment seeing the thousand-year-old monument brought back sense of time past. One blessing of such a pilgrimage, one joy of having come through, aches of the journey forgotten, shaken, into eyes.

*(May 8)*
crosspoints: *NE, NW, SW, SE*
*(724)*
*(762)*

*(701-56)*

69

それより野田の玉川・沖の石を尋ぬ。末の松山は寺を造て末松山といふ。松のあひあひ皆墓はらにて、はねをかはし枝をつらぬる契の末も、終はかくのごときと悲しさも増りて、塩がまの浦に入相のかねを聞。五月雨の空聊はれて、夕月夜幽に、籬が嶋もほど近し。蜑の小舟こぎつれて、肴わかつ聲々に、「つなでかなしも」とよみけん心もしられて、いとゞ哀也。其夜、目盲法師の琵琶をならして奥上るりと云ものをかたる。平家にもあらず舞にもあらず、ひなびたる調子うち上て、枕ちかうかしましけれど、さすがに邊土の遺風忘れざるものから、殊勝に覚らる。

70

## 24

Noda and the Oki-no-ishi. On Sue-no-Matsuyama temple
known as Masshōzan. Everywhere between pines graves, bringing home the fact that even vows of "wing and wing, branch
and branch, forever merging" must also come to such, sadness
increasing, and at Shiogama Beach a bell sounded evening.
A *samidare* sky cleared some, faint early moon, Magaki Island
also coming clear. "Fishing boats" pulling together, voices
dividing the catch, "the haul's excitement" grasped now,
rousing deep response. That night a blind minstrel played
*biwa* and chanted *Oku-jōruri*. Not like Tales of the Heike
nor *mai*, singing country tunes boisterously to our pillows, but
not unusual either, traditional in such out-of-the-way places,
and good they're kept up.

Sue-no-Matsuyama:
*Pine Mountain
Point*

(*May 9*)
samidare: *May rains*

biwa: *Japanese lute*

71

早朝塩がまの明神に詣。國守再興せられて、宮柱ふとしく彩椽きらびやかに、石の階九仞に重り、朝日あけの玉がきをかゝやかす。かゝる道の果塵土の境まで、神靈あらたにましますこそ、吾國の風俗なれといと貴けれ。神前に古き宝燈有。かねの戸びらの面に「文治三年和泉三郎寄進」と有。五百年來の俤、今目の前にうかびて、そゞろに珍し。渠は勇義忠孝の士也。佳命今に至りて、したはずといふ事なし。誠人能道を勤、義を守べし。「名もまた是にしたがふ」と云り。

## 25

gama Myōjin shrine. The *kokushu* had had it rebuilt, pillars immense, painted rafters resplendent, stone steps rising rather steeply, morning sun blazing vermilion-lacquered fence. As far as the road goes, to the very end of dusty earth, the unimaginable power of the gods persists and still answers each need, one of our country's traditions and to my mind most precious. Before the shrine a fine old lantern. On its metal door the inscription read:

*kokushu: in this case, Date Masamune*

*(1187)*

IN THE THIRD YEAR OF THE
BUNJI CONTRIBUTED BY
IZUMI SABURŌ

Images of five centuries floated before my eyes, making me feel, despite myself, strange. Here was a courageous loyal trustworthy warrior. To this day no one's not revered his name. Yes, man should follow the way of *jen* and stick to his principles. As they say, fame will follow, in turn, of itself.

*All night, thunder . . .*

日既午にちかし。船をかりて松嶋にわたる。其間二里餘、雄嶋の磯につく。

抑ことふりにたれど、松嶋は扶桑第一の好風にして、凡洞庭・西湖を恥ず。東南より海を入て、江の中三里、浙江の潮をたゝふ。嶋々の数を盡して、欹ものは天を指、ふすものは波に匍匐。あるは二重にかさなり三重に疊みて、左にわかれ右につらなる。負るあり抱るあり、兒孫愛すがごとし。松の緑こまやかに、枝葉汐風に吹たはめて、屈曲をのづからためたるがごとし。其氣色窅然として美人の顔を粧ふ。ちはや振神のむかし、大山ずみのなせるわざにや。造化の天工、いづれの人か筆をふるひ詞を盡さむ。

76

## 26

Hired boat and crossed to Matsushima. Distance of more than two *li*. Landed at Ojima Beach.

*(May 9)*
*"mulberry land:"*
*Chinese poeticism*
*for Japan*

Now, though it's been only too often observed, Matsushima presents a magnificent vista, the finest in our "mulberry land" and comparable to that of Lake Dōtei or Seiko. The sea enters at the southeast, three *li* wide at that point, like Sekkō at flood tide. All sorts of islands gather here, steep ones pointing to sky, others creeping upon waves. Or some piled double on each other, or even triple, and some divided at one end and overlapping at the other. Some bear others on their backs, some seem to embrace them, as if caressing their offspring. Green of the pines deep, needles and branches mauled by the salt winds—though contorted by nature—look artificially trained. The feeling: one of intense beauty, of a lovely creature engrossed in her glass. Perhaps in the Age of the Gods Ōyamazumi shaped this place. Who with brush or speech can hope to describe the work of heaven and earth's divinity?

*Ōyamazumi:*
*mountain god of*
*legend*

*Matsushima (ya . . .*

雄嶋が磯は地つゞきて海に出たる嶋也。雲居禪師の別室の跡、坐禪石など有。將、松の木陰に世をいとふ人も稀々見え侍りて、落穂・松笠など打けぶりたる草の庵閑に住なし、いかなる人とはしられずながら、先なつかしく立寄ほどに、月海にうつりて、昼のながめ又あらたむ。江上に歸りて宿を求れば、窓をひらき二階を作て、風雲の中に旅寐するこそ、あやしきまで妙なる心地はせらるれ。

　　　　　松嶋や鶴に身をかれほとゝぎす　　　曾良

　予は口をとぢて眠らんとしていねられず。旧庵をわかるゝ時、素堂松嶋の詩あり。原安適松がうらしまの和歌を贈らる。袋を解てこよひの友とす。且杉風・濁子が發句あり。

80

## 27

mainland, projects into the sea. There, ruins of Ungozenji's hut and *zazen* rock and other things remain. And there too amongst pines still seen religious recluses, several here and there, by thatched huts where twigs drop off, living quietly, it seemed, as smoke of leaves and pine-cones rose. And though unknown to me, they drew my heart/mind, moon now mirrored in sea, the day's view altered, renewed. Back on shore, put up at inn whose second-storey windows opened upon sea, feeling of resting on the journey now among wind and cloud, extraordinarily high.

zazen: *religious meditation*

> Matsushima (ya
> come as a crane
> *hototogisu*
> (Sora)

I, wordless, tried sleeping, but couldnt. On leaving my old hut Sodō had made me a poem about Matsushima. And Hara Anteki a *waka* about Matsu-ga-urashima. Undid my neckbag, let them be my company this night. And with them *hokku* from Sampū and Dakushi.

十一日、瑞岩寺に詣。當寺三十二世の昔、眞壁の平四郎出家して、入唐歸朝の後開山す。其後に雲居禪師の徳化に依て、七堂甍 改 りて、金壁荘 嚴光を輝、 仏土成 就の大伽藍とはなれりける。彼見仏 聖 の寺はいづくにやとしたはる。

## 28

priesthood: *i.e., to become a bonze*
Tō: *i.e., T'ang country, or China*
(*1610*)

This temple founded some thirty-two generations ago when Makabe-no-Heishirō entered the priesthood, upon returning from Tō. Later, influenced by Ungozenji's superior character, the seven main buildings, tiles newly refurbished, walls gilded, splendidly embellished, seem to have become the great edifice of the arrived-at Buddha Land. Wondered if temple of Kenbutsu Hijiri might also be seen.

十二日、平和泉と心ざし、あねはの松・緒だえの橋など聞傳て、人跡稀に、雉兎蒭蕘の往かふ道、そこともわかず、終に路ふみたがえて、石の巻といふ湊に出。こがね花咲とよみて奉たる金花山海上に見わたし、數百の廻船入江につどひ、人家地をあらそひて、竈の煙立つゞけたり。思ひがけず斯る所にも來れる哉と、宿からんとすれど更に宿かす人なし。漸まどしき小家に一夜をあかして、明れば又しらぬ道まよひ行。袖のわたり・尾ぶちの牧・まのゝ萱はらなどよそめにみて、遙なる堤を行。心細き長沼にそふて、戸伊摩と云所に一宿して、平泉に到る。其間廿余里ほどゝおぼゆ。

84

## 29

(*May 12*)

ON THE TWELFTH SETTING OUT FOR Hiraizumi via the celebrated Pine of Aneha and the Odae Bridge, found ourselves pursuing a path with few signs of life, only an occasional hunter or woodcutter passing, ended up, after wrong turn-off, at harbor-town called Ishi-no-maki. Mt Kinka, described in a poem to an emperor as "where gold blossoms," seen far over water and hundreds of cargo boats clustering inlet, human dwellings there contesting space, smoke curling up from ovens. Our unexpected arrival prompted immediate effort to procure lodgings, but nothing to be had. In the end found a corner in a shack for that night and at daybreak

(*May 13*)

off again on unknown paths. Saw Sode Ferry, Obuchi Meadows, Mano Reedflats from afar, following along a long embankment. Bypassed a dismal stretch of marshland and spent night at place called Toima and finally reached Hiraizumi. Distance covered, roughly, more than twenty *li*.

三代の榮耀一睡の中にして、大門の跡は一里こなたに有。秀衡が跡は田野に成て、金鶏山のみ形を殘す。先高舘にのぼれば、北上川南部より流るゝ大河也。衣川は和泉が城をめぐりて、高舘の下にて大河に落入。康衡等が旧跡は、衣が関を隔て南部口をさし堅め、夷をふせぐとみえたり。偖も義臣すぐつて此城にこもり、功名一時の叢となる。「国破れて山河あり、城春にして草青みたり」と笠打敷て、時のうつるまで泪を落し侍りぬ。

　　　夏草や兵どもが夢の跡

　　　卯の花に兼房みゆる白毛かな　　　曾良

　兼て耳驚したる二堂開帳す。經堂は三將の像をのこし、光堂は三代の棺を納め、三尊の佛を安置す。七宝散うせて、珠の扉風にやぶれ、金の柱霜雪に朽て、既頽廢空虚の叢と成べきを、四面新に囲て、甍を覆て風雨を凌。暫時千歳の記念とはなれり。

　　　五月雨の降のこしてや光堂

86

MAGNIFICENCE OF THREE GENERATIONS

"gone as in a sleep" and shambles of great outer gate one *li* this side of what was. Where Hidehira's seat was, now largely empty fields and only Mt Kinkei unchanged. Climbing to Takadachi discovered the Kitakami a large stream flowing from region of Nambu. The Koromogawa, encircling Izumi Castle, below Takadachi, empties into the larger stream. The ancient ruins of Yasuhira and others, with the Koromo Barrier between, fortifying entrance into Nambu, seem to have guarded against Ezo people. For all that, the faithful retainers, the elite, were confined to the castle, their moment of valiant effort so much grass. "The country devastated, mountains and rivers remain; in the castle in spring the grass green" remembered and we set our hats under us and sat there for a time and tears came.

> summer grass
> warriors
> dreams' ruins
> in *unohana*
> Kanefusa appearing
> whitehaired
>
> (Sora)

Two temple halls we'd heard of, open. The *kyōdō* contains images of the Three Generals and the *hikaridō* coffins of the three generations and enshrines the three images of Buddha. The Seven Gems now gone, jewelled doors rent by winds, gilded pillars fretted by frost and snow, would have all been long since destroyed and back to grass but for reinforced walls on four sides and a cover over the tiled roof against wind and rain. So it still stands, memorial of a thousand years past.

> May rains
> falling may have left
> *hikaridō*

Kinkei: *lit. "Golden Birds" (cock and hen)*
Takadachi: *"Hill (or High) Place"*

Ezo: *i.e. Ainu*

kyōdō: *sutra library*
images: *wooden statues*
hikaridō: *lit. "Hall of Splendor" (built 1124)*

*summer grass . . .*

南部道 遙にみやりて、岩手の里に泊る。小黒崎・みづの小嶋を過て、なるごの湯より尿前の関にかゝりて、出羽の國に越んとす。此路旅人稀なる所なれば、関守にあやしめられて、漸 として関をこす。大山をのぼつて日既 暮ければ、封人の家を見かけて舎 を求む。三日風雨あれて、よしなき山中に逗留す。

蚤虱馬の尿する枕もと

31

ways off, stayed over at village of Iwade. Went on via
*(May 15)*   Ogurozaki, Mizu-no-ojima, and from Narugo Hot Springs
made for the Shitomae Barrier and on over into province
of Dewa. This route few travellers ever take, so guards eyed
us suspiciously and barely let us through. Climbed high mountain there, sun already down, and happening on a border-
guard hut sought shelter there. For three days winds and rain
fierce, forced to hang on in that dull retreat.

> fleas lice
> horse pishing
> by the pillow

あるじの云、是より出羽の國に大山を隔て、道さだかならざれ
ば、道しるべの人を頼て越べきよしを申。さらばと云て人を頼侍れば、究竟の若者反脇
指をよこたえ、樫の杖を携て、我々が先に立て行。「けふこそ必あやうきめにもあふ
べき日なれ」と、辛き思ひをなして後について行。あるじの云にたがはず、高山森々とし
て一鳥聲きかず、木の下闇茂りあひて夜る行がごとし、雲端につちふる心地して、篠の中
踏分踏分、水をわたり岩に蹴て、肌につめたき汗を流して、最上の庄に出づ。かの案内
せしおのこの云やう、「此みち必不用の事有。恙なうをくりまいらせて仕合したり」と、
よろこびてわかれぬ。跡に聞てさへ胸とゞろくのみ也。

## 32

MAN AT THE HUT SAID, "FROM HERE to Dewa, with a high mountain to cross and the trail far from clear, better get a guide to take you over." So we hired a man, a strapping young fellow who looked like he could take care of himself, with curved short-sword at hip and oaken staff in hand, and on he took us. Felt like just the day to sort with danger and with some fear followed after. As the man said, the mountain was high and thickly wooded, beyond bird cry, in deep forest darkness like groping about at night. Felt as if dirt were tumbling from overloaded clouds, pushed pushed on through *shino* brush, waded water, stumbled rock, drenched in cold sweat, came out at last in region of Mogami. Our guide then said, "Generally it's not so easy along this trail. Glad we made it this time without any adventures." And contentedly left us. But we, even hearing this afterwards, found our hearts beating faster.

shino: *small bamboo*

(*May 17*)

尾花澤にて清風と云者を尋ぬ。かれは富るものなれども、志いやしからず。都にも折々かよひて、さすがに旅の情をも知たれば、日比とゞめて、長途のいたはり、さまざまにもてなし侍る。

　　　涼しさを我宿にしてねまる也
　　　這出よかひやが下のひきの聲
　　　まゆはきを俤にして紅粉の花
　　　蠶飼する人は古代のすがた哉　　　曾良

94

33

AT OBANAZAWA VISITED MAN CALLED
Seifū. Well-to-do but not a petty mind. And from frequent
trips to Miyako well appreciates how wayfarers feel, had us stay
many days to rest up after being so much on the go, entertained
us in a host of ways.

cool
being right at home
spr-rawling

come on out
from under the worm room
croaker

the eyebrow brush
so resembling
safflower

silkworm tending
folk antique
in mode
(Sora)

95

*May rains* . . . hikaridō

山形領に立石寺と云山寺あり。慈覺大師の開基にして、殊清閑の地也。一見すべきよし、人々のすゝむるに依て、尾花沢よりとつて返し、其間七里ばかり也。日いまだ暮ず。麓の坊に宿かり置て、山上の堂にのぼる。岩に巖を重て山とし、松柏年旧、土石老て苔滑に、岩上の院々扉を閉て物の音きこえず。岸をめぐり岩を這て仏閣を拜し、佳景寂寞として心すみ行のみおぼゆ。

　　閑さや岩にしみ入蟬の聲

98

## 34

(*May 27*)

IN THE DEMESNE OF YAMAGATA THE mountain temple called Ryūshakuji. Founded by Jikaku Daishi, unusually well-kept quiet place. "You must go and see it," people urged; from here, off back towards Obanazawa, about seven *li*. Sun not yet down. Reserved space at dormitory at bottom, then climbed to temple on ridge. This mountain one of rocky steeps, ancient pines and cypresses, old earth and stone and smooth moss, and on the rocks temple-doors locked, no sound. Climbed along edges of and crept over boulders, worshipped at temples, penetrating scene, profound quietness, heart/mind open clear.

> quiet
> into rock absorbing
> cicada sounds

最上川のらんと、大石田と云所に日和を待。爰に古き誹諧の種
こぼれて、忘れぬ花のむかしをしたひ、芦角一聲の心をやはらげ、此道にさぐりあしして、
新古ふた道にふみまよふといへども、みちしるべする人しなければと、わりなき一卷残しぬ。
このたびの風流爰に至れり。

　最上川はみちのくより出て、山形を水上とす。ごてん・はやぶさなど云おそろしき難所有。
板敷山の北を流て、果は酒田の海に入。左右山覆ひ、茂みの中に船を下す。是に稲つみたる
をやいな船といふならし。白糸の瀧は青葉の隙々に落て、仙人堂岸に臨て立。水みなぎつて
舟あやうし。

　　　五月雨をあつめて早し最上川

## 35

INTENDING TO RIDE DOWN THE MO-
gamigawa, waited at a place called Ōishida for good weather.
Here the seeds of old *haikai* sown, brought back past times and
unforgotten flowers, cry of a reed-flute easing heart, gone
astray trying to take both ways at once, the new and the old,
no one to guide them, left them a collection of no great merit.
But as far as *fūryū* had till then come.

The Mogamigawa has its source in Michinoku and its upper
reaches in Yamagata. With the daunting perils of the Goten
shoals and Hayabusa rapids. Descending north of Mt Itajiki,
it empties into sea at Sakata. Right, left, mountains close, up,
boat shot down through clustering trees. Boats like this with
sheaves of rice probably those called *inabune*. The Shiraito Falls
plunges through thick green foliage and the Sennindō stands
at river's brink. What with swollen waters, boat ran risks.

collection: *i.e.,*
*a renka, composed*
*at a party there*

Goten: *i.e., "scat-*
*tered* go (*chess*)
*stones"*
Hayabusa: *lit.*
*"swooping falcon"*

Shiraito:
*"White-thread"*

> May rains
> gathering swift
> Mogamigawa

六月三日、羽黑山に登る。圖司左吉と云者を尋て、別當代會覚阿闍利に謁す。南谷の別院に舍して、憐愍の情こまやかにあるじせらる。

四日、本坊にをゐて誹諧興行。

　　　有難や雪をかほらす南谷

五日、權現に詣。當山開闢能除大師はいづれの代の人と云事をしらず。延喜式に羽州里山の神社と有。書寫、黑の字を里山となせるにや。羽州黑山を中略して羽黑山と云にや。出羽といへるは、鳥の毛羽を此國の貢に献ると風土記に侍とやらん。月山・湯殿を合て三山とす。當寺武江東叡に属して、天台止觀の月明らかに、円頓融通の法の灯かゝげそひて、僧坊棟をならべ、修験行法を勵し、灵山灵地の験効、人貴且恐る。繁榮長にしてめで度御山と謂つべし。

36

(*June 3*)

THIRD DAY OF THE SIXTH MOON, climbed Haguroyama. Visited Zushi Sakichi and received in audience by the *bettō-dai*, Egaku Ajari. Lodged at side-temple at Minamidani and he eagerly and cordially welcomed us.

bettō-dai: *deputy intendant at temple*
Minamidani: *South Valley*

The fourth, at main temple building, *haikai* party.

> thank *you*
> perfuming snow
> Minamidani

(*June 5*)
Gongen: *avatar of Buddha in Ryōbu Shinto*
Nōjo Daishi: (*shd be Taishi) 3rd prince of Emperor Sushun (588–92)*
Dewa: lit. *"feather-bearing"*

On the fifth worshipped at Gongen temple. Its founder, Nōjo Daishi, but date unknown. In the *Engishiki* given as shrine of Ushūsatoyama (羽州里山). Whoever did the copying wrote "satoyama" (里山) for "kuro" (黒) by mistake probably. One of the Ushūkuroyama *kanji* dropped out and so it became Haguroyama (羽黒山) probably. The idea of Dewa seems clarified in the *Fudoki*, where payments in down and feathers are mentioned as a form of local tribute. Gassan and Yudono with it compose a trinity. This temple affiliated with Tōei

Bukō: *Edo area*

in Bukō, the moon of the Tendai *shi-kan* clear, way of *endon-yuzū*, light increased, ridge to temple ridge extending, the devout encouraging each other in austere duties, the grace revealed (*genkō*) in heart's mountains and heart's land calls forth reverence and awe in folk. Prosperity unconfined and the mountains may be said to bestow blessings.

*May rains . . . Mogamigawa*

八日、月山にのぼる。木綿しめ身に引かけ、寶冠に頭を包、強力と云ものに道びかれて、雲霧山氣の中に氷雪を踏でのぼる事八里、更に日月行道の雲関に入かとあやしまれ、息絶身こゞえて、頂上に臻れば日没て月顯る。笹を鋪、篠を枕として、臥て明るを待。日出て雲消れば湯殿に下る。

谷の傍に鍛冶小屋と云有。此國の鍛冶、靈水を撰て爰に潔斎して釼を打、終月山と銘を切て世に賞せらる。彼龍泉に剣を淬とかや。干將・莫耶のむかしをしたふ、道に堪能の執あさからぬ事しられたり。岩に腰かけてしばしやすらふほど、三尺ばかりなる桜のつぼみ半ばひらけるあり。ふり積雪の下に埋て、春を忘れぬ遅ざくらの花の心わりなし。炎天の梅花爰にかほるがごとし。行尊僧正の歌の哀も爰に思ひ出て、猶まさりて覚ゆ。惣而此山中の微細、行者の法式として他言する事を禁ず。仍て筆をとゞめて記さず。坊に歸れば、阿闍闍の需に依て、三山順礼の句々短冊に書。

　　　涼しさやほの三か月の羽黑山

　　　雲 の 峯 幾 つ 崩 て 月 の 山

　　　語られぬ湯殿にぬらす袂かな

　　　湯殿山銭ふむ道の泪かな　　　曾良

106

# 37

*(June 8)*
yūshime: *paper garland often worn by mt. priests*
hōkan: *cotton head-gear with pointed ends*
gōriki: *lit. "strong power:" mountain guide, probably* yamabushi

EIGHTH, CLIMBED GASSAN. YŪSHIME hanging from our necks, heads covered by *hōkan*, led by a *gōriki*, up into mountain air, clouds, mist, walking ice and snow, going some eight *li* up until it seemed near the gateway to the clouds, sun and moon passing over, each breath a last one, numb, reached peak, sun down, moon out. Spread bamboo grass, used *shino* as pillows, lay down, waited for daybreak. Sun up, clouds gone, headed down towards Yudono.

At valley's edge place known as the Swordsmiths' Hut. Smiths in these parts fetch holy water here to purify themselves and to temper blades in which they eventually carve: Gassan: a mark of wide repute. Said that swords were tempered at the Ryūsen too. Reminiscent of ancient Kanshō and Bakuya. That their dedication to their craft not superficial, wellknown. Perched on rock resting a while, saw half-opened buds of three-foot cherry trees. Buried under piled-up reluctant snow, slow blossoms dont forget spring, remarkable stubbornness. As if the "plum under blazing heaven" were suddenly seen here. Recalled Gyōson Sōjō's poem, which made buds seem to bud the more. By and large against code to disclose what goes on here. And with that the brush stops, wont write. Went back to dormitory and at the Ajari's instance wrote poems of our visit to the Three Mountains on *tanzaku*.

-san: *mountain (i.e., temple)*

cool ah
faint crescent's
Haguro-san

clouds' peaks
how many collapsing
moon's mountain

prohibited speech
at Yudono wetting
my sleeve

Yudono-yama
penny stepping-stones
and tears
                    (Sora)

羽黒を立て鶴が岡の城下、長山氏重行と云物のふの家にむかへられて、誹諧一巻有。左吉も共に送りぬ。川舟に乗て酒田の湊に下る。淵庵不玉と云醫師の許を宿とす。

　　　あつみ山や吹浦かけて夕すゞみ

　　　暑き日を海にいれたり最上川

108

## 38

(*June 13*)

LEFT HAGURO AND AT CASTLE town of Tsuru-ga-oka received by Nagayama Shigeyuki at his

round: *i.e.*, renka

place and composed a round of *haikai* there. Sakichi, who had come this far, saw us off. Went by river-boat down to harbor of Sakata. Stayed at En-an Fugyoku, the doctor, 's house.

Atsumi: "*Hot Sea*"
Fuku-ura: "*Windy Harbor*"

from Mount Atsumi
over to Fuku-ura
evening's cooling

hot sun
into the sea driven
Mogamigawa

江山水陸の風光数を盡して、今象潟に方寸を責。酒田の湊より東北の方、山を越礒を傳ひ、いさごをふみて、其際十里、日影やゝかたぶく比、汐風眞砂を吹上、雨朦朧として鳥海の山かくる。闇中に莫作して、雨も又奇也とせば、雨後の晴色又頼母敷と、蜑の苫屋に膝をいれて雨の晴を待。

　其朝、天能霽て、朝日花やかにさし出る程に、象潟に舟をうかぶ。先能因嶋に舟をよせて、三年幽居の跡をとぶらひ、むかふの岸に舟をあがれば、「花の上こぐ」とよまれし桜の老木、西行法師の記念をのこす。江上に御陵あり、神功后宮の御墓と云。寺を干滿珠寺と云。此處に行幸ありし事いまだ聞ず。いかなる事にや。

110

## 39

and mountains, land and sea, for eyes, the heart's inch-space
now bounded towards Kisakata. From Sakata harbor north-
east, crossing mountains, following shore, walking sand, some
ten *li*, sun falling, sea wind swirling grit, gusty rain hid Mt
Chōkai. Groping through darkness, maybe rain "an enchantment" anyhow and later clearing like a charm, maybe, and
so squeezed into a fisherman's shanty to wait till the wet let up.
Next morning, sky utterly clear, sun miraculous, dazzling,
boated about Kisakata. First headed for Nōin Island, prayed
at what of his three years' retreat remains, then over to op-
posite shore and found the old cherry tree—"over whose
blossoms [fishermen] row"—memorializing Saigyō-Hōshi. At
water's edge an imperial tomb said to be Jingū Kōgū's. Temple
there known as Kanmanjuji. Never heard of Empress
visiting it. How come?

(*continued*)

(*June 16*)

Jingū Kōgū: *empress,*
d. 269

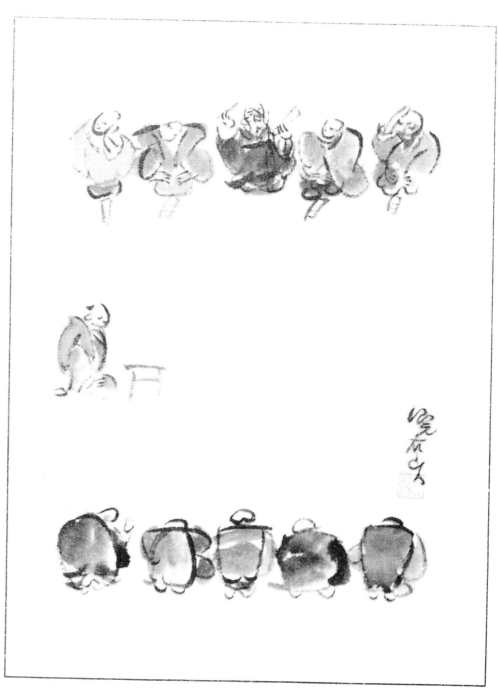

*thank* you . . .

此寺の方丈に座して簾を捲ば、風景一眼の中に盡て、南に鳥海天をさゝえ、其陰うつりて江にあり。西はむやむやの関路をかぎり、東に堤を築て秋田にかよふ道遙に、海北にかまえて浪打入る所を汐ごしと云。江の縦横一里ばかり、佛松嶋にかよひて又異なり。松嶋は笑ふが如く、象潟はうらむがごとし。寂しさに悲しみをくはえて、地勢魂をなやますに似たり。

　　　象潟や雨に西施がねぶの花
　　　汐越や鶴はぎぬれて海涼し
　　　（祭礼）
　　　象潟や料理何くふ神祭　　　曾良
　　　蜑の家や戸板を敷て夕涼　　　みのゝ國の商人低耳
　　　（岩上に雎鳩の巣をみる）
　　　波こえぬ契ありてやみさごの巣　　　曾良

114

hōjō: *10 ft. square chamber (front room) in Zen temple*

Sitting in temple *hōjō*, rolling up blinds, eyes held the scene: to south Chōkai supporting heaven, its image resting in water.

West the Muyamuya Barrier obstructs and east along a built-up embankment, road to Akita far off, sea to north shel-

Shiogoshi: *"tide flooding"*

tering, and just where the tide rolls in, place called Shiogoshi. From one end to other and out again bay's about a *li*, superficially resembling Matsushima, but with a certain difference. Matsushima seems to smile, whereas Kisakata seems aggrieved. Tinge of the sad in its isolatedness, nature here like a troubled spirit.

> Kisakata (ya
> in rain Seishi
> silk-tree blossoms
>
> Shiogoshi (ya
> crane leg splashed
> sea cool
>
> (The Festival)
> Kisakata (ya
> what's to eat's
> divine feast
> > (Sora)
>
> fisherman's home
> panels laid out
> evening's cooling
> > (Teiji: Merchant of Mino)
>
> (On Finding an Osprey's Nest on a Rock)
> waves do not undo
> the vow vowed there
> osprey's nest
> > (Sora)

115

酒田の余波日を重て、北陸道の雲に望、遙々のおもひ胸をい
たましめて、加賀の府まで百卅里と聞。鼠の関をこゆれば、越後の地に歩行を改て、越中
の國一ぶりの関に到る。此間九日、暑濕の勞に神をなやまし、病おこりて事をしるさず。

　　　文月や六日も常の夜には似ず

　　荒海や佐渡によこたふ天河

116

## 40

ing up, seeing clouds above the Hokuroku district. Mind aches,
the distance, hearing it's a hundred and thirty *li* to Kaga City.
Crossed the Nezu Barrier, starting fresh into Echigo, reached
the Ichiburi Barrier in Etchū. During this stretch of nine days
putting up with heat and rain, spirit sore afflicted, taken ill, no
way to keep up writing.

Nezu: *"Mouse"*
(*June 25*)

> even the sixth
> of poetry's month's
> night unusual
>
> wild seas (ya
> to Sado shoring up
> the great star stream

**117**

今日は親しらず・子しらず・犬もどり・駒返しなど云北国一の難所を越てつかれ侍れば、枕引よせて寐たるに、一間隔て面の方に、若き女の聲二人計ときこゆ。年老たるおのこの聲も交て物語するをきけば、越後の國新潟と云所の遊女成し。

伊勢參宮するとて、此関までおのこの送りて、あすは古郷にかへす文したゝめて、はかなき言傳などしやる也。白浪のよする汀に身をはふらかし、あまのこの世をあさましう下りて、定めなき契、日々の業因いかにつたなしと、物云をきくきく寐入て、あした旅立に、我々にむかひて、「行衞しらぬ旅路のうさ、あまり覺束なう悲しく侍れば、見えがくれにも御跡をしたひ侍ん。衣の上の御情に、大慈のめぐみをたれて結縁せさせ給へ」と泪を落す。「不便の事には侍れども、我々は所々にてとゞまる方おほし。只人の行にまかせて行べし。神明の加護かならず恙なかるべし」と云捨て出つゝ、哀さしばらくやまざりけらし。

　　　　一家に遊女もねたり萩と月

曾良にかたれば書とゞめ侍る。

118

**41**

shirazu, Koshirazu, Inumodori and Komagaeshi, amongst the
most dangerous spots in Hokkoku and named accordingly,
worn out by it, pulled up pillows and bedded down for
night, only to catch sounds of voices in front room one
room away, sounding like two young women. Old man's
voice mingled with theirs as stories told are heard and it seemed
they were play-girls from Niigata in Echigo Province. On their
way to the Ise Shrines and the man seeing them off as far as the
Barrier, heading back next morning with notes of theirs
and usual greetings home. " 'On the strand where white
waves crash' we wander, children of the sea, thus fallen, to
every chance relation, every day *karma*, shame. . .," heard
and more, drifting off; next day, departing, they came over,
tearfully, saying: "We dont know which way we're supposed
to go and feel so uncertain and helpless, could we just follow in
sight of your footsteps. By the grace of your robes, please grant
us the blessing of your mercy and the providence of Buddha."
"Unfortunately we often like to take detours. Just follow anyone
going your way. Surely the gods will protect you and see you
safely through," words left them on leaving, but felt sorry for
them for some time after.

> in the one house
> play-girls also slept
> *hagi* and moonlight

Sora hearing this wrote it down.

Hokkoku: *North Country*

play-girls: *literal; often translated "prostitutes," but misleading in many ways*

くろべ四十八が瀬とかや、数しらぬ川をわたりて、那古と云浦に出。擔籠の藤浪は春ならずとも、初秋の哀とふべきものをと、人に尋れば、「是より五里いそ傳ひして、むかふの山陰にいり、蜑の苫ぶきかすかなれば、蘆の一夜の宿かすものあるまじ」といひをどされて、かゞの国に入。

　　　わせの香や分入右は有磯海

## 42

THE KUROBE KNOWN FOR ITS FORTY-eight rapids and we did have to cross no end of water-ways to get to bay called Nago. Though not spring and feeling, in fact, of early fall pervasive, waves of wistaria at Tako suggested a visit and asking the way were told: "From here it's five *li* along the coast, then over the mountain there—not much more than a handful of fishermen's huts, a night's lodging even in the reeds hard to find," enough to scare us off; so on into province of Kaga.

> early rice fragrance
> pushing thru to right
> the "Rough Sea"

121

　　　　　　卯の花山・くりからが谷をこえて、金沢は七月中の五日也。爰に大坂よりかよふ商人何處と芸者有。それが旅宿をともにす。

　一笑と芸ものは、此道にすける名のほのぼの聞えて、世に知人も侍しに、去年の冬早世したりとて、其兄追善を催すに、

　　　　　　塚も動け我泣聲は秋の風

ある草庵にいざなはれて

　　　　　　秋涼し手毎にむけや瓜茄子

途中吟

　　　　　　あかあかと日は難面もあきの風

122

## 43

*(July 15)*

the art: *that of* haikai

of Kurikara, in Kanazawa on mid-fifth of the seventh moon. Kasho, a merchant from Osaka, in town. Stayed at same inn. One Isshō, known for his devotion to the art, of some repute too in the world outside, died unexpectedly this past winter quite young and his elder brother was now conducting memorial services:

> tomb move too
> my cry's
> autumn's wind

On being invited to a thatched hermitage:

> fall coolness
> hand by hand preparing
> eggplants cucumbers.

And on the road this poem:

> red red
> sun unrelentingly
> autumn's wind.

小松と云所にて

　しほらしき名や小松吹萩すゝき

　此所太田の神社に詣。眞盛が甲・錦の切あり。往昔、源氏に属せし時、義朝公より給はらせ給とかや。げにも平士のものにあらず。目庇より吹返しまで、菊から草のほりもの金をちりばめ、龍頭に鍬形打たり。眞盛討死の後、木曽義仲願狀にそへて此社にこめられ侍よし、樋口の次郎が使せし事共、まのあたり縁紀にみえたり。

　　むざんやな甲の下のきりぎりす

## 44

Komatsu: *"Small
Pine" or "Young
Pine"*
(*July 25*)

AT A PLACE CALLED KOMATSU:

delicately
named Komatsu blowing
*hagi/susuki.*

nishiki: *imperial
brocade*

Visited Tada Shrine here. Sanemori's helmet and part of its
*nishiki* there. In days of old, presented to him, as a member of
the Genji, by his commander Yoshitomo, it is said. Clearly
not designed for a common soldier. From eye-cover to ear-flap
engraved with chrysanthemums interlaced by ivy scrollwork,
a dragon headpiece with hoe-shaped frontlets attached. After
Sanemori's death in battle, Kiso Yoshinaka with message of
prayer donated it to shrine, Higuchi Jirō his emissary: can see
them there even now as annals of shrine describe.

cruel!
under the helmet
cricket

125

山中の温泉に行ほど、白根が嶽跡にみなしてあゆむ。左の山際に観音堂あり。花山の法皇三十三所の順礼とげさせ給ひて後、大慈大悲の像を安置し給ひて、那谷と名付給ふと也。那智・谷組の二字をわかち侍しとぞ。奇石さまざまに、古松植ならべて、萱ぶきの小堂、岩の上に造りかけて、殊勝の土地也。

　　　石 山 の 石 よ り 白 し 秋 の 風

## 45

Kannondō:
  temple to goddess
  (god) of mercy
  (986)
Daiji Daihi: *Goddess*
  *(God) of Great*
  *Mercy*

kaya: *zebra grass*

at Yamanaka saw as we went Mt Shirane just behind. At foot of mountain to left a Kannondō. The retired Emperor Kazan, after pilgrimage to the Thirty-Three Temples, had an image of Daiji Daihi enshrined here and named the place Nata, it is said. The name, it is also said, comes from *kanji* taken from *N*achi and *T*anigumi. All kinds of oddshaped rocks abound and ancient pines amongst them; small *kaya*-thatched temple there, handsomely situated.

> Ishiyama
> stones no whiter
> autumn's wind

127

*even the sixth . . .*

温泉に浴す。其功有明に次と云。

　　　　山中や菊はたおらぬ湯の匂

　あるじとする物は、久米之助とていまだ小童也。かれが父誹諧を好み、洛の貞室若輩の
むかし爰に來りし比、風雅に辱しめられて、洛に歸て貞徳の門人となつて世にしらる。功
名の後、此一村判詞の料を請ずと云。今更むかし語とはなりぬ。

　曾良は腹を病て、伊勢の国長嶋と云所にゆかりあれば、先立て行に、

　　　　行々てたふれ伏とも萩の原　　　曾　良

と書置たり。行ものゝ悲しみ、殘ものゝうらみ、隻鳬のわかれて雲にまよふがごとし。予
も又

　　　　今日よりや書付消さん笠の露

130

## 46

BATHED AT THE HOT SPRINGS. THEIR
efficacy said to be nearly up to Ariake's.

> Yamanaka(ya
> leave *kiku* unplucked
> redolent water

kiku: *our unwieldy*
*word, chrysanthe-*
*mum*

(*d. 1675*)
Raku: *old word for*
*Kyoto, or a section*
*of it*

judge: *i.e., of a*
haikai *contest*

Our host here, known as Kumenosuke, a mere lad, whose
father doted on *haikai* and who so embarrassed Teishitsu of
Raku when he visited here as a young man at the art that when
he returned to Raku he became a disciple of Teitoku and thus
gained renown. Because of the earlier occasion, however, when
he later came as judge, they say, he refused payment here.
This has already become legend.

Sora, stomach ailing, went off to relatives at Nagashima in
Ise, writing down:

> walking on and on
> though stricken quite
> *hagi* fields.

wild geese: *an*
*allusion from Chinese*
*poetry*

Pain of one who goes, emptiness of one left behind, like
the parting of a pair of wild geese, lost in clouds. And I too:

> from this day forth
> efface the inscription
> *kasa*'s dew.

131

大聖持の城外、全昌寺といふ寺にとまる。猶加賀の地也。曾良
も前の夜、此寺に泊て、

          終宵秋風聞やうらの山

と残す。一夜の隔千里に同じ。吾も秋風を聞て衆寮に臥ば、明ぼのゝ空近う讃經聲すむま
まに、鐘板鳴て食堂に入。けふは越前の国へと、心早卒にして堂下に下るを、若き僧ども
紙硯をかゝえ、階のもとまで追來る。折節庭中の柳散れば、

          庭掃て出ばや寺に散柳

とりあへぬさまして草鞋ながら書捨つ。

132

## 47

STAYED JUST OUTSIDE THE CASTLE town of Daishōji at the Zenshōji. Still in Kaga country. Sora at this temple only last night and left here:

> all night long
> hearing fall winds
> the mountain behind.

A single night feels like a thousand *li*. I heard fall winds too, resting in temple dormitory, and towards daybreak voices chanting sutras clearer, gongs, and went to refectory. Today had to be off into Echizen country and with that in mind hurrying from the temple, young priests came hurrying down the steps after me with paper and ink-slab. At that moment willows in the yard were shedding leaves:

ink-slab: *shallow ink dish, usually of stone*

> sweeping the yard
> let me leave the temple
> the willows' failings.

Sandals already on, jotted it hastily down for them.

越前の境、吉崎の入江を舟に棹して汐越の松を尋ぬ。

終宵嵐に波をはこばせて
　月をたれたる汐越の松　　西　行

此一首にて数景盡たり。もし一辨を加るものは、無用の指を立るがごとし。

## 48

AT BOUNDARY OF ECHIZEN, INLET OF
Yoshizaki, hired a boat there for the pines of Shiogoshi.

all night long . . .:
  *poem attributed to*
  *Saigyō*

all night long
storm-fraught waves
moon dripping
Shiogoshi's pines

In this one poem are the various feelings of the place expressed.
To add to it would be just pointing one finger too many.

*wild seas (ya . . .*

丸岡天龍寺の長老、古き因あれば尋ぬ。又金沢の北枝といふもの、かりそめに見送りて、此處までしたひ來る。所々の風景過さず思ひつゞけて、折節あはれなる作意など聞ゆ。今既別に望みて、

物書て扇引さく余波哉

五十丁山に入て永平寺を礼す。道元禪師の御寺也。邦機千里を避て、かゝる山陰に跡をのこし給ふも、貴きゆへ有とかや。

138

## 49

(Aug 11?)

VISITED THE VENERABLE ELDER OF Tenryūji at Maruoka, renewing old acquaintances. And Hokushi from Kanazawa also, who'd—as it happened—seen me this far and now reluctantly turned back. His way of mulling and noting what eyes see of various places often quite sensitive, now facing departure:

> what was composed
> on the fan wrenched apart
> subsides together.

50 chō: *abt. 3.2 mi.*
"a thousand li from Hōki:" *from Chinese Book of Odes;* Hōki: *imperial seat; here implying Kyoto*

Went off fifty *chō* into mountains to pray at Eiheiji. Dōgenzenji's temple. To have situated it beyond such mountains "a thousand *li* from Hōki" was, as they say, the result of careful consideration.

139

福井は三里 計 なれば、夕飯したゝめて出るに、たそがれの路たどたどし。爰に等栽と云古き隠士有。いづれの年にか江戸に來りて予を尋。遙十とせ餘り也。いかに老さらぼひて有にや、將死けるにやと人に尋侍れば、いまだ存命してそこそこと敎ゆ。市中ひそかに引入て、あやしの小家に夕皃・へちまのはえかゝりて、鷄頭・はゝ木々に戸ぼそをかくす。さては此うちにこそと、門を扣ば、侘しげなる女の出て、「いづくよりわたり給ふ道心の御坊にや。あるじは此あたり何がしと云ものゝ方に行ぬ。もし用あらば尋給へ」といふ。かれが妻なるべしとしらる。むかし物がたりにこそかゝる風情は侍れと、やがて尋あひて、その家に二夜とまりて、名月はつるがのみなとにとたび立。等栽も共に送らんと、裾おかしうからげて、路の枝折とうかれ立。

140

## 50

*(Aug 11–12 or 12–13?)*

and after supper struck out for it, the way as darkness came on no mean trick for feet. Old recluse called Tōsai living here. When was it he came to call on me in Edo? More than ten years already. Has he turned senile now or is he dead? Told upon enquiring: "Still alive," living at such and such a place. Quiet spot off the road a piece, modest weather-beaten house, all entangled in *yūgao* and *hechima* and the door lost behind *keitō* and *hahakigi*. Well, this must be it, and knocked at door, bringing a humble woman out. "Where does the reverend *gobō* come from? The master of the house has gone to Mr So-and-so's, not far from here. If you want him, please look for him there," she said; seemed to be his wife. Looking like someone straight out of legend, and at once went off after him, found him and stayed two nights at their house, leaving again then for the full moon at Tsuruga harbor. Tōsai, tucking up his *kimono* in a funny sort of way, cheerfully decided to come along and serve as a guide-post.

yūgao and hechima: *kinds of gourds*
keitō: *cock's comb*
hahakigi: *broom cypress*
gobō: *Buddhist priest, bonze*

kimono: *simply "clothing," but Japanese style*

141

漸 白根が嶽かくれて、比那が嶽あらはる。あさむづの橋をわたりて、玉江の蘆は穂に出にけり。鸎の関を過て湯尾峠を越れば、燧が城、かへるやまに初鴈を聞て、十四日の夕ぐれつるがの津に宿をもとむ。その夜、月殊晴たり。「あすの夜もかくあるべきにや」といへば、「越路の習い、猶明夜の陰晴はかりがたし」と、あるじに酒すすめられて、けひの明神に夜參す。仲哀天皇の御廟也。社頭神さびて、松の木の間に月のもり入たる、おまへの白砂霜を敷るがごとし。「往昔、遊行二世の上人大願發起の事ありて、みづから草を刈、土石を荷ひ泥淳をかはかせて、參詣往來の煩なし。古例今にたえず、神前に眞砂を荷ひ給ふ。これを遊行の砂持と申侍る」と、亭主のかたりける。

　　　月清し遊行のもてる砂の上

十五日、亭主の詞にたがはず雨降。

　　　名月や北國日和定なき

51

Mt Hina emerged. Crossed the Asamuzu Bridge, the reeds at Tamae flourishing, through the Uguisu Barrier, via the Yuno-o Pass, the Castle of Hiuchi, at Mt Kaeru heard first wild geese cry, and on evening of the fourteenth at Tsuruga harbor found lodging at inn. That night the moon especially bright. "Think it'll be like this tomorrow night?" "Hard to tell about weather in Koshiji. Might be fine and then again might be overcast," and after some *sake* from innkeeper, paid night visit to the Kehi Myōjin. Monument to Emperor Chūai. Certain solemnity about shrine, moon through pines touched white sand before edifice as if with frost. In days of old Yugyō Shōnin the 2nd undertook the immense project of making access for visitors much easier, himself helped cut grass, lug earth and rocks, drain marshes. Nor has the old custom yet stopped and sand is still carried to shrine. "Known as *Yugyō-no-sunamochi*," innkeeper explained.

Kaeru: *"Return"* (*Aug 14*)

(*r. 192–200?*)

Yugyō-no-suna-mochi: *Yugyō-sandcarrying*

> moon clear
> Yugyō carried carrying
> sand cover

The fifteenth, just as innkeeper predicted, it rains.

> harvest moon
> Hokkoku weather
> don't depend on it

143

*in the one house . . .*

十六日、空霽たれば、ますほの小貝ひろはんと、種の濱に舟を走す。海上七里あり。天屋何某と云もの、破籠・小竹筒などこまやかにしたゝめさせ、僕あまた舟にとりのせて、追風時のまに吹着ぬ。濱はわづかなる海士の小家にて、侘しき法花寺あり。爰に茶を飲酒をあたゝめて、夕ぐれのさびしさ感に堪たり。

　　　寂しさや須磨にかちたる濱の秋
　　　浪の間や小貝にまじる萩の塵

　其日のあらまし、等栽に筆をとらせて寺に殘す。

146

## 52

warigo: *divided lunch box*
sasae: *bamboo bottle for* sake

Hokke: *Buddhist sect*

SIXTEENTH, SKY CLEARING, DECIDED to gather small shells, sailed along Iro Beach. Altogether seven *li*. One Tenya So-and-so, with carefully-packed *warigo* and *sasae*, etc., taking servants along for the ride, enjoying tailwinds arrived in good time. Only a few fishermen's huts along beach and bedraggled Hokke temple nearby. Here drank tea, hot *sake*, much moved by the pervading sense of isolatedness at nightfall.

> isolation
> more overwhelming than Suma
> beach's fall

> between wave and wave
> mingling small shells
> *hagi* dust

Had Tōsai take the brush and set down major events of the day, to leave at the temple.

147

*. . . Tōsai living here.*

露通も此みなとまで出むかひて、みのゝ国へと伴ふ。駒にた
すけられて大垣の庄に入ば、曽良も伊勢より來り合、越人も馬をとばせて、如行が家に入集
る。前川子・荊口父子、其外したしき人々日夜とぶらひて、蘇生のものにあふがごとく、且
悦び且いたはる。旅の物うさもいまだやまざるに、長月六日になれば、伊勢の迁宮おがまん
と、又舟にのりて、

　　蛤のふたみにわかれ行秋ぞ

53

(*September 3–6?*)

ROTSŪ HAD COME TO THE HARBOR TO meet me and came along into Mino. Reached the demesne of Ōgaki by horse, Sora having also come in from Ise and Etsujin come galloping in, got together at Jokō's house. Zensenshi, Kciko father and sons, as well as other friends, day and night, kindly called, as if encountering someone restored to life, showing their pleasure and warm affection. Before fully recovering from the exhaustion and exertion of the long journey, on the sixth day of *Nagatsuki*, decided to visit the ceremonial rebuilding at Ise, back in the boat again,

Nagatsuki: *lit. "long month, or moon"*

> clam
> shell and innards parting
> departing fall.

151

跋　　　　　　　　　　からびたるも、艶<sub>えん</sub>なるも、たくましきも、はかなげなるも、お
くの細みちみもて行<sub>ゆく</sub>に、おぼえずたちて手たゝき、伏<sub>ふし</sub>て村肝<sub>むらぎも</sub>を刻<sub>きざ</sub>む。一般は簑をきるきるかかる旅せまほしと思<sub>おもひ</sub>立<sub>たち</sub>、一<sub>ひと</sub>たびは坐してまのあたり奇景をあまんず。かくて百般<sub>ひやくばん</sub>の情<sub>じやう</sub>に、
鮫人<sub>かうじん</sub>が玉を翰<sub>ふで</sub>にしめしたり。旅なる哉、器<sub>うつは</sub>なるかな。只なげかしきは、かうやうの人のい
とかよはげにて、眉の霜<sub>（お）</sub>のをきそふぞ。

　　　　元祿七年初夏　　　　　　　　　　　　　　　　　　　　　　　素　龍　書

152

*Most texts of the* Oku-no-hosomichi *close with the famed calligrapher Soryū's "Epilogue." It was he, at B's call, who copied out the version from which we and all readers today draw sustenance. In 1694.* Kōjin *refers to the weaverdemon of China, whose tears turn into jewels.*

# EPILOGUE

THE DRY TONE AND RICH SUPPLE VIG-
orous style keep me immersed in reading the *Oku-no-hosomichi*,
sometimes arising and clapping or lying down, stirred to the
core. Once had my raincoat on, eager to go on ; like journey,
and then again content to sit imagining those rare sights. What
a hoard of feelings, Kōjin jewels, has his brush depicted! Such a
journey! Such a man! A pity only that he turns wearier and
more and more white comes tingeing his brows.

*written by Soryū*
*(early summer,*
*seventh year of the Genroku).*

153

# NOTES

THE BIOGRAPHY OF BASHŌ (1644–94) IS AVAILABLE most succinctly and accurately, as far as it goes, in *Haikai and Haiku*, published by The Nippon Gakujutsu Shinkōkai, Tokyo, in 1958. And all the various terms relating to *haiku* are adequately explained in the same volume. There is no lack of books on the subject in English now, in any event, and the interested reader will have no trouble finding information. Enough to note here that the *Oku-no-hosomichi* is the last of the travel journals and regarded as the most mature of them. Bashō was, as a youngster, in the service of a feudal lord, chiefly as attendant to the lord's son (Tōdō Yoshitada), who died unfortunately—though perhaps fortunately for us— at the age of 22. This led to B's removing himself boldly from the Yoshitada household and into a much more independent life. He had already been attracted to poetry as well as to contemplative religion. First living in Kyoto, till about age 28, thereafter—apart from journeys—largely in Edo (Tokyo). His pen-name (family name Matsuo), Bashō, was drawn from the plantain tree near the hut he lived in—about age 37—provided him by Sampū. Evidently the tree's "uselessness" (in a manner reminiscent of Taoism) was the key-factor in leading to his taking the name.

The travel journal was a well-established Oriental tradition. By the time Bashō was ready to compose the *Oku-no-hosomichi* he had become

157

very aware of its possibilities. He projects with unusual economy of force the fulness of his life and sensibility, and the resonance of that life and sensibility reaches us yet.

The original text, the Soryū version, is unpunctuated, though there are natural clear syntactic units. Bashō's syntax, however, though often frowned upon by latterday Japanese grammarians for its lack of rule, is curious, characteristic and exact. We have tried not to improve upon it.

The notes could be hopelessly voluminous. We have preferred to offer only what additional word is immediately illuminating or stimulating, and a few points are elaborated to give some sense of a depth involved throughout that might not otherwise be fully realized. The reader may assume that when Bashō uses "standard locutions" (like brushing the cobwebs off his hut) he does so for a sense of relation with past literary usage and for the concrete values he feels anew. Allusions are everywhere, often in single words. They were not as remote as, say, those in *The Wasteland* are to most of us. They were expected to be grasped at once by any likely reader of that time: no one was expected to apply to an encyclopedia or thesaurus. Certain key anthologies—notably the *Wakanrōeishū*, half of which was Chinese classical poetry—were highly popular with the middle classes and certainly much poetry was current and remembered.

It may also be worth reminding the reader that Bashō didnt, in effect, *write* poetry, but made it—spoke it, aired it. *Haiku* were easily carried in the head: the formalities of the structure (and you see Japanese today ticking off the syllables as they try to recall some) were a great help. Bashō wasnt, in short, sitting at a desk writing. The poems were made often on the spur of the moment and for specific occasions. By the time they were incorporated in works like this one, of course, they had undergone revision. Certainly reconsideration. And Bashō, conscientious as always and with more at stake than his followers, would not have inserted any work that seemed to him inferior. It follows, then, that the poems by Sora and others are well-regarded by the master, providing thematic counterpoint and accompaniment, and not for the sake of making Bashō's poems look better.

Sam: Johnson has noted (in his *Preface to Shakespeare*, 1765): "Parts are not to be examined till the whole has been surveyed; there is a kind of intellectual remoteness necessary for the comprehension of any great work in its full design and in its true proportions; a close approach shows the smaller niceties, but the beauty of the whole is discerned no longer."

**TITLE**

The title of the journal: The *Oku-no-hosomichi*, literally means: Oku's Narrow Path(-s). Oku is the region north and west of Edo (Tokyo). In Bashō's day it was considered rather remote and off the beaten track. But the Narrow Path also refers to a specific road that travellers generally followed in passing through the region. The word "strait" may be more apt than "narrow." The title suggests to the Japanese mind the deep and difficult way. The way thru life. The *selva oscura*, perhaps.

Cf. Bruno Snell: *Discovery of the Mind*, p. 304—"Callimachus was the first to introduce the proud rejection of vulgarity into poetry. We now know this chiefly from the prologue to the *Aitia*. He does not want to travel on the broad highway thronged by others, but on his own path, however narrow."

**INTRODUCTION**

"*When tears come . . . :*" cf. Leopardi's letter (of 20 Feb. 1823): "I went to visit the tomb of Tasso and wept there. This is the first and only *pleasure* I have felt in Rome. . . ." A contemporary poet, an American travelling in the traditional scenes of Europe (Louis Zukofsky, *Four Other Countries* (1956–57)) writes: " . . . Liveable/place; whose character is/endurable// As the eyes are moist before/the regularly spaced/flower window boxes/ of Berne . . . ," and cf. in Lévi-Strauss's (Eng. *The Savage Mind*) quote of T.G.H. Strehlow: "The Northern Aranda (Australia) clings to his native soil with every fibre of his being. He will always speak of his own 'birthplace' with love and reverence. Today, tears will come into his eyes when he mentions an ancestral home site . . . . Mountains and creeks and springs and water-holes are, to him, not merely interesting or beautiful scenic features . . .; they are the handiwork of ancestors from whom he himself has descended. . . . The whole countryside is his living, age-old family tree . . . ."

**1**

*Moon & Sun . . .* : the opening words allude to writing of Li Po (701–62). Often translated as "Months and days . . . " (which the words also mean)—but these terms seem inadequate. Dr DT Suzuki shares our opinion. It may not be irrelevant to point out that Plato in the *Timaeus* (38C ff.) in referring to the revolvings of moon and sun mentions that the word *planet* (a Greek word) means "wanderer." And Leopardi a century or more after B could see the moon also as a "wandering" figure.

*many that perished:* B has in mind his favorites, Saigyō (1118–90), itinerant priest-poet famous for his *waka* (in *Shinkokinshū*: Kamakura anthology), whose trail B largely follows; Sōgi (1421–1502), priest-poet noted for work in *renka*, and a major influence on B; the Chinese poets Li Po and Tu Fu—like most T'ang poets in government service "on the road." The reader should understand that Bashō's health at the outset has been on the wane, so that his speculation about dying on the journey is not idle, nor romantic. And the fact that the journal was composed *after-wards*, when B's health was even more clearly declining, aware that he *didnt* die on the journey, underlines the aches involved, quietly. Out of the worst B will make the best.

*Barrier:* (Japanese *seki*); these were border checkpoints, mounted by guards. Already identification-papers (so common were political incursions) were the order of the day in Japan and had been for some centuries past. Pilgrims and itinerant actors usually had an easier going of it, but were also natural disguises.

*Dōsojin:* Japanese counterpart of Hermes. God of wayfarers, with carved stone markers at roadsides, bridges, etc. Against diseases and/or evil spirits. Also divine link between living and dead.

*Sampū:* (1647–1732) patron and disciple of B. Wealthy fish-merchant. Sampū's summer house, it may be noted, was only 500 yards or so from the earlier dwelling. Any man of means in the Edo area would provide himself with several homes for reasons as practical as frequent fires and mistresses.

*the grass door:* the poem is evidently expressing, under the general theme of transiency, a proportion that reads: Matsushima is to Sampū's summer house as that was to the "grass door" hut. The "dolls' house" provides (3rd March) a clear seasonal note of the *Hina matsuri* (girls' festival) when dolls, usually of imperial proportions, are carefully posted in tiers on an altar.

*omote:* opening page of a *renka* (linked verses).

**2**

*YAYOI:* old term for March, literally "time for growing." All the old lunar

160

names have exact relation to rice-farming: the staple Japanese foodstuff. Constant of the landscape.

*"a waning moon . . . :"* from the Hahakigi section of the *Genji Monogatari*.

*Senju:* a well-known jumping-off point on the road to Oku and a fishing center at the confluence of streams just north of Edo.

*departing spring:* the poem, apart from its allusion to Chinese poetry, suggests Sampū, the fish-merchant, who must have been amongst the company bidding the travellers farewell (there would have been a party of sorts) and the "birds" suggest the wanderers-to-be.

*fishes'/eyes tears:* alluding to a poem by Tu Fu (712–70), as does the exaggerated sense of distance preceding.

### 3

*Genroku:* period (1688–1703), Tokugawa shōgunate. Time of relative freedom and well-being in Japan, at least in the centers. Cf. Saikaku, Chikamatsu, and the flourishing art of *ukiyo-e*.

*"under Go skies:"* Go is Japanese reading of Chinese *Wu;* remote area evoking images of snow and old age. Linked to poetry by Po Chü-i (772–846) or Li Tung (end of 9th c). (Achilles Fang)

*hanamuke:* Johnson in *A Journey to the Western Islands* (1773–5) writes: "it is not to be imagined without experience, how in climbing crags, and treading bogs, and winding through narrow and obstructed passages, a little bulk will hinder, and a little weight will burthen; or how often a man that has pleased himself at home with his own resolution, will, in the hour of darkness and fatigue, be content to leave behind him every thing but himself."

### 4

*Konohana Sakuya Hime:* legendary princess; lit., "princess who causes flowers to bloom." Daughter of Ōyamatsumi-no-kami, the mountain god. To prove, although pregnant, she was not unfaithful to her newlywed divine husband, Prince Ninigi, sealed herself in the Utsu-muro (exitless room) and set fire to it. Out of this ordeal Prince Hohodemi was born: the name meaning "appearing out of fire."

*konoshiro:* (*Konosius punctalus*), fish of about 7–8 inch length generally, found mostly in the Inland Sea today. Fish when burnt has odor of cremated body and was substituted for a girl once in a rather similar fix to our princess (cf. Iphigeneia in Taurus). Literally the word means "in place of a child."

### 5

*jen:* Confucian term. Cf. Pound's version of the *Analects*. Relating analogously: *vir* and *virtu*. I.e., manfulness, clear-spirited, etc.

### 6

*Kūkai Daishi:* (774 or 5—834 or 5), sometimes known as Kōbō Daishi, founder of Shingon sect (Buddhist). High priest, famous for calligraphy (said to have invented *hiragana* syllabary), poetry and religious works.

*eight directions:* cf. Waley's version of a poem by T'ao Chien (*Chinese Poems,*

161

p. 107): "The lingering clouds, rolling, rolling/And the settled rain, dripping,/In the Eight Directions—the same dusk. . . . "

*the four classes:* under feudal rule: warrior, farmer, artisan, merchant.

**7**

*Mt:* in this journal and generally the word "yama" is translated "mountain" or "Mount," though often the western eye would say "hill." The feeling, however, is in terms of local scale and mountain is more apt.

*changing apparel:* in lunar reckoning seasonal changes of clothing customarily occurred on Apr 1st and Oct 1st. In *haikai* the ref. is to spring. As for name-changing, even today done by some priests and artists.

*Sora:* (1649–1710), about 1689 definitively affiliated with B. His poems tend to be much slighter than B's, but clearly "felt" and "point" particularities.

*to a waterfall confined:* religious ascetics used frequently to stand immersed in a waterfall as an "exercise" in late spring/early summer.

**8**

*kasane:* as explained in poem, the flower's name and a curious, but attractive, rural-type name. Cf. our "Daisy" or "Myrtle."

**9**

*Inuoümono:* this refers to a "sport" indulged in by warriors of Heian and Kamakura times. Dogs, corralled by bamboo fencing, were shot at by warriors riding by with bow and arrow. A form of archery practice gone out of fashion as missiles and targets have improved.

*Tamamo-no-mae:* Japan's (via China) famous fox-lady. (We only have "vixens.") The details of her story are told in the Noh, *Sesshōseki.* "-mae," is a fem. honorific, like "lady."

*Shō-hachiman:* warrior deity, with shrines found in various parts of Japan.

*Yoichi:* one of Minamoto Yoshitsune's (i.e., of the Genji) heroic warriors. The story told in the *Heike Monogatari:* an incident at the battle of Yashima of unusual prowess in archery.

*Shugen-Kōmyōji:* the reader will realize that the ending *-ji* in such place names refers to "temple," as *-yama* or *-san* means mountain or mount; *-gawa* is river or stream.

*ashida:* high rain clogs. Here likely referring specifically to those kept on an altar at the shrine and considered En-no-gyōja's (founder of Shugendō sect; i.e., religious asceticism, *yamabushi* tribe). They would be worshipped as strength-giving in the art of long-distance walking.

**10**

*Butchō-oshō:* (1641–1715), B's Zen master.

*-oshō:* B uses religious titles for individuals which are untranslatable into Christian terms. We have preferred to keep them and so at least cue the reader to distinctions. -Hōshi: bonze (Dharma master).

*the ten views:* a way of saying—having wandered about the temple precincts (landscaped gardens): 5 bridges 10 views is the landscaping formula.

*Myōzenji:* or *Genmyōzenji* (1239–1296). *-zenji:* Chinese *ch'an-shih;* Ch'an

162

(Zen) master, lived 15 years in a secluded cave, much sought out for teachings. Cave-names given by the dwellers themselves remain suggestive.

*Hōun-Hōshi:* (467–529), in Chinese, *Fa-yün Fa-shih.* Chinese high priest, who towards end of his life built a hermitage in or against a rock-cave, where disciples arrived for chatter. (AF)

## 11

*Sesshōseki:* still exists, though fenced about. The legends associated with it told in Noh of the same name.

## 12

*willow of the "pacing stream:"* refers to a *waka* by Saigyō; cf. Noh play *Yugyō-yanagi,* which also touches on the Shirakawa Barrier in the next section.

## 13

*"somehow sending word . . . :"* quote from a *waka* by Taira Kanemori.

*Three Barriers:* variously identified, but the Shirakawa-seki most made of in poetry. *"Autumnal winds:"* from a *waka* by Nōin-Hōshi; *"the maple"* from a *waka* by Yorimasa.

*Kiyosuke:* (1104–1177). Of the Fujiwara. Late Heian poet. Referring to Takeda Kuniyuki's donning court robes at the Barrier in deference to the poem by Nōin mentioned above. Cf. Jouvenel, *Sovereignty,* p. 103: "Investiture . . . consists in clothing a man anew in robes which are at once pure and majestic."

*Sora's haiku:* gaily alludes to all that precedes.

## 14

*Tōkyū:* (1638–1715). The local *haikai* man. Six years older than B. Had met in Edo. Much revered in his area.

*fūryū:* (lit. "wind-fluent") untranslatable term. B's uses of it in this journal define it. Reflective of Japanese taste for the natural and immediate and humble as well as evanescent, as grace-full.

*waki and daisan: renka* terms. The opening 5–7–5 syllable poem in a *renka* is the *hokku;* the second, 7–7, the *waki* (cf. *waki* role, side-kick, in Noh); the third, 7–5–7, the *daisan.*

## 15

*"in mountain depths . . . :"* alluding to a poem by Saigyō. Cf. *Chuang-tzu,* Bk. 24, v. 14.

*the Western Paradise:* Buddhist allusion, locale of Amitabha (the Measureless Light), one of the great Buddhist incarnations.

*Gyōgi Bosatsu:* (668 or 670–749). High priest in the Nara period, Korean by birth (cf. Chapter 8, *Japanese Buddhism,* Sir Charles Eliot, for an extended account). *Bosatsu* (Boddhisattva) an honorary title conferred upon him by the Emperor Shōmu (724–748).

## 16

*Mt Asaka:* like all place-names, apart from post-towns, B has some allusion to poetry in mind, as well as often an interest in the original sense of the name.

163

*katsumi:* (*Zizania latifolia*), in B's day two plants by this name: water-oat and iris. Former more likely here. *hana-* means "flower," so the same plant in blossom. *Katsumi* used in thatching especially for Boys' Day (May 5th): in old calendar midsummer's start.

*Kurozuka cavern:* lit. Black Cave, legendary home of a demon in the guise of an old woman. Cf. Noh play of the same name.

**17**

*Shinobu-mojizuri:* (*Davallia bullata*) is a local grass used for rubbing dye into cloth placed on a famous granitic rock. Favorite way of creating a fresh and natural design in the region. Word *shinobu* also, as a verb, means: "recalling times past." And it was believed that this particular rock when rubbed with young plants would reveal the image of one's beloved.

**18**

*Satō Shōji:* Satō Motoharu. *Shōji:* title of manor official (secretary-in-chief). His two sons, Tsugunobu and Tadanobu, lost their lives in defending that of their lord Yoshitsune. Their wives to comfort their mother-in-law put on the men's warrior gear as if in triumphal return. The story finds reference in the Noh drama, *Settai*.

*the story of their heroism:* Cf. Johnson again in his travels with Boswell (which have many interesting overlays with Bashō's journal and the differences also tell much): "To abstract the mind from all local emotion would be impossible, if it were endeavoured, and would be foolish, if it were possible. Whatever withdraws us from the power of our senses; whatever makes the past, the distant, or the future predominate over the present, advances us in the dignity of thinking beings. Far from me and from my friends, be such frigid philosophy as may conduct us indifferent and unmoved over any ground which has been dignified by wisdom, bravery, or virtue. That man is little to be envied, whose patriotism would not gain force upon the plain of *Marathon*, or whose piety would not grow warmer among the ruins of *Iona!*"

*Weeping Rock:* at Mt Ken in China, named by poet Tu Yu, for a famous tomb there which, merely to look upon, it was said, caused one to weep.

*Minamoto Yoshitsune:* (1159–1189). Perhaps the most celebrated of Japanese warriors, of the Genji clan. The stories, which are legion, may be found in the *Heike Monogatari* especially and in various Noh and Kabuki plays (cf. A & G Halford, *The Kabuki Handbook*, pp 418–25 for summary).

*Benkei:* priest of the Kamakura period, famous as one of Yoshitsune's cleverest and most devoted followers. Occurs in various Noh and Kabuki pieces. (v. Halford, *op. cit.*)

*paper standards:* alludes to paper carp, etc., seen flying above houses in Japan where families have sons (May 5th festivity—though they are "out" several weeks in advance generally).

**19**

*the usual trouble:* diagnosed as diarrhoea, though other guesses (piles, etc.) have been made.

164

*fleas mosquitoes . . . :* cf. *Chuang-tzu:* Bk. 14 with its counsel in the face of such—"see that naturalness is not lost, move with the wind."

**20**

*Abumizuri:* good example of how B uses placenames literally: "stirrup-rubbing" (rock): evidently a narrow pass and a "strait is the gate" feeling.

*district of Kasashima:* an example of B's probably deliberate errors. The district was, in fact, that of Natori. But in terms of feeling, sound and over-all structure, B is "right."

*Tō-no-chūjō Sanekata:* (d. 998?). *Tō-* refers to Fujiwara clan. Famous as poet and lover of Sei Shōnagon of *Pillow-Book* fame (cf. Waley). Exiled for insulting celebrated court calligrapher, Fujiwara-no-Yukinari. Known in exile as Lord of Mutsu. (In Oku.)

*susuki grass of memory:* sedge planted at Sanekata's grave and mentioned in poem by Saigyō.

**21**

*Nōin-Hōshi:* (988–1050). Priest, then poet. Heian period. Influenced recluse literature, later established by Saigyō. Considered one of the 36 great poets of his period.

*Kyohaku:* (?–1696). Disciple. Some selected poems in the *Minashiguri* (Hollow Chestnut) anthology.

**22**

*Day of plaiting eaves:* formerly done on Boys' Day.

*blue flags:* (Japanese *ayamegusa*), of the iris family, evidently auspicious and indicative of strength and virility. Actually more nearly magenta in color.

*asebi: Pieris japonica* (azalea family).

All place-names from poetry.

*"Attendants, an umbrella . . . :"* quoted from the *Kokinshū* (famous anthology of Heian period: cf. Keene, *Anthology of Japanese Lit.*).

*Yakushidō:* famous shrine built by the feudal lord of Sendai, Date Masamune (1565–1636).

*Tenjin Shrine:* dedicated to priest and scholar Sugiwara Michizane (845–903). Built in 974. He was exiled in life and deified as Tenjin, with a temple in most Japanese towns. (Cf. Eliot, *op. cit.*, p. 183n.)

*ah . . . :* cf. Pound's CANTO IV: "Saffron sandal so petals the narrow foot" (based on Catullus LXI: "huc veni nives gerens/luteum pede soccum."

**23**

*Tsubo-no-ishibumi:* oldest extant monument in Japan, erected in 712.

*Ōno-no-ason Azumabito:* (d. 742). Military leader under three Emperors. Vanquished Ezo people and built Taga Castle. Titles italicized mean: *inspector* and *governer-general.*

*sangi and setsudoshi:* councillor (cabinet member) and commander of the defense of the

*Tōkai:* Eastern Sea (15 provinces of Tōkaido) and

*Tōzan:* Eastern Mountain Region (13 provinces of Tōzandō).

**24**

*Oki-no-ishi:* a rock, in water, celebrated in poetry.

*Sue-no-Matsuyama:* pine-clad slope near the sea; in fact, the sea from above seems to flow around its base. Famous love poems related to it. Section full of images of fidelity.

*"wing and wing, branch and branch . . . :"* derive from Chinese poetry: Po Chü-i (772–843) as picked up via *Genji Monogatari.*

*"Fishing boats . . . :"* from anonymous (?) poem in the *Kokinshū,* mentioning Shiogama (lit. "salt pot").

*Oku-jōruri:* dramatic back-country balladry, accompanied by *biwa* or *shami-sen* (Japanese mandolin), telling of Yoshitsune's coming to the Eastern provinces.

*mai:* or *Kōwaka-mai:* a sort of simplified Noh dance, originating in the Ashikaga period (after Kamakura), but in B's day much on the wane.

**25**

*Izumi Saburō:* of the Fujiwara, third son of Hidehira, brother of Yasuhira, who was responsible for Yoshitsune's death. Killed by his brother also, for being loyal to the famed leader (at age 23).

**26**

*Dōtei:* Lake Tung-t'ing in Hunan province (China). *Seiko:* Hsi-hu (-*hu:* large lake, in Chinese) in the city of Hangchow. Lit. "West Lake." Famed spots. (AF). There is a famous painting by Mu Ch'i of *Dōtei* in autumn and Okakura in his *Book of Tea,* p. 98, writes of: ". . . Linwo-sing, losing himself amid mysterious fragrance as he wandered in the twilight among the plum blossoms of the Western Lake" (favorite images of Chinese landscape in Japanese eyes).

The description of Matsushima suggests the array of rocks and/or shrubs in Zen gardens.

*Sekkō:* Che-chiang: i.e., the Ch'ien-t'ang River in Chekiang Province, China. Famous for its tidal bore. (AF).

**27**

*Ungozenji:* under patronage of Date Tadamune (son of Masamune), restored the Zuiganji temple. Monk of famous probity and religious influence (1583–1659).

*crane:* image of longevity and good omen.

*Sodō:* (1642–1716). Studied *haikai* with Kigin (1624–1705), B's teacher, in Kyoto, but finally settled in Edo and became friendly with B.

*Hara Anteki:* Edo doctor. Well-versed in *waka.*

*Dakushi:* pen-name of warrior who while on duty in Edo got to know B.

**28**

*Zuiganji:* Tendai temple originally in Hōjō (1205–1333) period, re-established as Rinzai.

*Makabe-no-Heishirō:* (?–1273), said to have visited China to study Ch'an Buddhism for 9 yrs. Lived in Matsushima thereafter.

166

*Kenbutsu Hijiri:* famed Buddhist priest of 12th c. (d. aged 82): lived on Ojima. (*Hijiri:* saint or sage or mahatma.) Saigyō met him once at the sage's cave in Noto and later, much impressed, visited him at Matsushima.

**29**

*pine of Aneha:* continually replanted. First celebrated in the *Ise Monogatari* (cf. Keene, *op. cit.*), where the pine is regarded as a woman.

*Odae Bridge:* from love poem in the *Goshūishū* (1086) and *Genji Monogatari*. *Odae* lit. means "breaking off life."

"*where gold blossoms:*" (gold first found in 749 in Oku) quoted from poem by Ōtomo-no-Yakamochi for the Emperor, in the *Manyōshū* (vol. 18, no. 4097).

*Sode:* lit. "sleeve." A tearful allusion from *Shin Gōshūishū* in mind.

*Obuchi:* alludes to a plaintive love-poem in the *Gosenshū* (951).

*Mano:* alludes to poem no. 396 in the *Manyōshū*, where a sense of distance is emphasized.

**30**

*three generations:* of the Fujiwara clan (1094–1189). But not associated with the famous Heian family. Hidehira the last of the three. Said to be of Ainu descent. Hidehira's son, Yasuhira, defeated by Minamoto-no-Yoritomo, the *shōgun* at Kamakura, though the former at Yoritomo's conspiratorial instance had killed Yoshitsune, Yoritomo's refugee brother.

" . . . *as in a sleep:*" alluding to the Noh play *Kantan:* with its ref. to the dreamed-of-imperial career of the Chinese scholar, Lu-sheng.

"*The country devastated . . . :*" adapted from a famous poem by Tu Fu.

*Kanefusa:* 63 when he died, loyally, with his lord Yoshitsune, when the castle at Takadachi was taken.

*Three Generals:* the statues (of wood) are, in fact, of Buddhist deities—but not unusually configuring particular people; here: Kiyohira, Motohira, and Hidehira.

*three images of Buddha:* Amida-Nyorai, Kannon and Seishi Bosatsu. (A-N: Shaka, as world-teacher; Amida, savior). (Kannon: figure of Mercy or Compassion; Seishi: Mahâsthâmaprâpta, Chinese: Ta–Shi–Chih, cf. Eliot, *op. cit.*, pp. 128–9, etc.)

*The Seven Gems:* (or "treasures") usually given as: gold, silver, crystal, white and red corals, and emerald (cf. *Sutra of Everlasting Life*).

**31**

*Ogurozaki:* allusion to poem in the *Kokinshū*, including ref. to *Mitsu-no-kojima:* "Three Isles," suggesting B thinks of friends left behind.

*suspiciously:* cf. *Chuang-tzu*, Bk. 13, v. 60.

*fleas lice:* cf. Martin Buber on *The Teaching of the Tao:* "Lao-tzu says to Khung-tsu: 'as horseflies keep one awake the whole night, so this talk of love of mankind and righteousness plagues me. Strive to bring the world back to its original simplicity.'" (Which also can be referred to No. 19).

**32**

*beyond bird cry:* suggested by poems of Tu Fu and Wang An-shih (1021–86).

**33**

*Seifū:* (1651–1721). Studied *haikai* in Kyoto with Teitoku school, but pupil at this point and admirer of B. Wealthy cosmetic (*beni*-dye) merchant. *Beni* (safflower), source of Japanese rouge. Obanazawa its usual locale.

*worm room:* of course, the silkworm; the "croaker" being the humble demon, the frog.

*antique:* women working at silkworm care evidently behaved and dressed (quite plainly) in a fashion reminiscent of a simpler more antique time. Readers often fail to note B's unfailing interest in the female element: it is a grace-note throughout and gives richness to the whole.

**34**

*Jikaku Daishi:* (Ennin, during his lifetime) (794–864). Tendai leader of his day, who had studied Buddhism 9 yrs in China (from 838), sympathetic to Shingon and Amidism (cf. Eliot, *op. cit.*)

**35**

*seeds of old haikai:* ref. to the Teimon (Teitoku) school or Danrin (Sōin) school, B's own "new" superseded all.

*reed-flute . . . :* alluding to Mongols in Chinese poetry, whose plaintive instruments made distant listeners feel how far from home they were.

*inabune:* lit. "rice-boat," sheaves of feudal tithings carried in them, but also ref. to the negative of antique times implied in the pun of "ina-:" a poem in the *Kokinshū* connects it also with the Mogamigawa. A love-poem, but its hesitant negative here suggests B's apprehension shooting the rapids.

*Sennindō:* lit. "hermit's hall:" alluding to Yoshitsune's retainer, Hitachibō Kaison's dwelling (now shrine), where he retired as a mountain hermit after the battle with the Heike. Figure of longevity: B's mention of it almost a prayer.

**36**

*Zushi Sakichi* (pen-name: Rogan): poet and dyeing-merchant for *yamabushi* clothing.

*Ajari* (Skt. âcârya): meaning "teacher" (cf. rabbi) or "master," priestly degree in Tendai and Shingon sects.

*Perfuming snow:* suggests a passage in the Confucian *Li Chi* (*Book of Rites*): "The perfumed wind comes from the South" and implies a warm and gracious atmosphere, as well as refreshing clarity.

*Engishiki:* 50-volume compilation of local rites and customs completed under the Emperor Daigo, 927.

*Fudoki:* Records of the Natural Features of the various imperial provinces, prepared at the instance of the Empress Gemmyō, 712. Some are still extant.

*shi-kan:* (Chinese: Chih-kuan; Skt: Samatha and Vipassanâ, i.e., calm and insight) central doctrine of the Tendai sect (cf. Eliot, *op. cit.*, pp. 334–5). Based on a work by Chih I (538–597), written in 594, Chinese founder of the T'ien-t'ai sect. Essentially Indian thought. A quote by Eliot, who admits his inability to grasp it, may illuminate the doctrine a little: (from

168

Chih I) "A bright mirror take as illustration. Brightness is *k'ung*: image *chia*: the mirror *chung*. Not joined, not divided: combined and separate just as they are."

The "trinity" (or "triad") of temples suggests the "three truths" of the Tendai sect: *Isshin Sangan*, as exemplified above and requiring preparation, training and concentration.

*endon-yuzū*: Tendai doctrine implying sudden and utter enlightenment, the light one carries and the light of the moon suddenly merging in a complete sphere.

**37**

*Gassan*: lit. "Moon Mountain." Highest of the mountains of traditional sanctity given here.

*Ryūsen*: lit. "Dragon Spring," reputed to have existed in South China.

*Kanshō and Bakuya*: two (another: *Lung-yüan*: B doesn't mention) swords famed in Chinese legend; in Chinese: *Kan-chiang* and *Mo-yeh*. The first, male; the second, female. (AF) cf. *Chuang-tzu*, Bk. 23, sect 8 (Legge), fn 2. Cf. the Noh play *Kokaji*.

*slow blossoms*: cf. the tea-master Rikyū's poem often quoted for its "wabi" quality (in the *Book of Tea*): "For those desiring flowers/Let me show/The full-blown spring/That dwells within/The struggling buds of/Snow-clad hills."

*"plum . . . blazing . . .:"* suggestive of *satori*. Allusion to a poem by Wang Wei (701–61), famed Chinese poet.

*Gyōson Sōjō*: (?–1135) Buddhist priest-poet, of the Minamoto family. Poem referred to, speaks of the isolation of mountain cherry blossoms. From the *Kinyōshū* (1125).

*the code*: unwritten rule, not to write or speak of what goes on or is seen there, etc., on religious premises.

*"at Yudono . . . :"* mountain's name lit. means "bath room." And "wetting one's sleeve" the indirect phrase of tears. One feels the exceeding release of feeling here, cleansing.

*penny stepping-stones*: Sora refers to the custom there of not picking up the goodluck largesse bestowed by pilgrims at the mountain site. They evidently form a trail to the temple. S's poem sounds almost humorous after B's—but no less devout for that.

**38**

*Nagayama Shigeyuki*: (pen-name, Jūkō) samurai poet, met B in Edo, disciple.

*En-an Fugyoku*: (?–1697) a disciple evidently, but this is the clearest ref. to him there is.

**39**

*heart's inch-space*: Chinese phrase. Cf. Lu Chi's *Wen Fu* (*New Mex. Quarterly*, Autumn 1952): "We lock infinity into a square foot of silk; pour a deluge from the inch-space of the heart." Cf. n. 3. (pp. 173–4) of Coomaraswamy's *The Transformation of Nature in Art*: "immanent space of the heart:" *antar-hrdaya-ākāsa*: space in the heart; i.e., inmost core of being.

*Seishi:* (Chinese: *Hsi-shih*) famous Chinese beauty of antiquity. Referred to in the poem "maybe rain an enchantment . . . " by Su Tung-p'o (Su Shih) (1036–1101) B quotes above. Cf. Blyth, *Haiku*, Vol. 3, p. 303.

*silk-tree blossoms:* (tree of mimosa family), but the Japanese word "nemu-no-hana" has a play on the verb *nemu*, "to sleep." In fact, the leaves fold shut at night. Pale orange blossom.

*what's to eat . . . :* Sora refers to the local festival of its tutelary god Myōjin, where no meat or fish are eaten. Festival normally falls on the 8th day of the 8th lunar month.

*panels:* the fishermen would remove the doors of their huts in summer (like all such elements in Japanese houses, grooved rather than hinged, and easily removable) and picnic on them.

*vow vowed:* EP's "fish-hawk" in Ode no. 1 in *The Classic Anthology*. (Cf. Legge, *Chinese Classics*, Vol. 4, p. 3, fn. to Ode no. 1) (AF). The bird, as Sora tells, nests on rocks close to the tide and remains faithful to his brood even in the teeth of it.

**40**

*poetry's month . . . :* July, old calendar. Eve of the Tanabata Festival: story of the star-couple, poems written of stars, hung in trees.

*wild seas:* cf. Tu Fu (*Poems of the Late T'ang*, Graham, Penguin, p. 46): "After sudden rain, a clear autumn night./On golden waves the sparkle of the Jewelled Cord./The River of Heaven white from eternity. . . . "

*Sado:* famed island off the West coast of Honshū, where many political exiles were sent; *the great star stream:* lit. "Heaven's river" is our Milky Way.

**41**

place-names of sentiment: *Oyashirazu:* lit. "parent lost;" *Koshirazu:* "child lost;" *Inumodori:* "dog turning back;" *Komagaeshi:* "horse turned back." Singular may be plural in Japanese. Only eyes can tell.

*"On the strand . . . :"* from the *Shinkokinshū*. Cf. Ortega y Gasset's description of the female element in Cervantes' *Exemplary Tales:* "worn-out, wandering young ladies who sigh deeply in the rooms of inns and speak of their maltreated virginity in Ciceronian style."

*By the grace of your robes:* B and S evidently mistaken for monks, but B's *haiku* becomes a prayer in their behalf, as well as a recognition of joined world. Note how B rings changes on the word *"hagi"* throughout the journal. (Also the most commonly mentioned flower, though or because simple, in the *Manyōshū*, occurring, it is said, no less than 138 times!) The shrines at Ise, it might be noted, were a famous excuse for young lovers to escape their families and find rendezvous.

*in the one house:* this poem, with its brief note by Bashō: "Sora hearing this wrote it down," has implications. Apparently B was shy of keeping it himself. It also corroborates two facts: 1) that B composed his poems aloud often, or simply in his head and 2) that the journal was edited and prepared afterwards. That B reconsidered and put the poem in

170

bespeaks particular affection for it. Extending it beyond any mere vulgarity.

*hagi:* usually translated as "bush-clover," recently introduced for improved ecology into US agriculture.

**42**

*waves of wistaria:* alluding to poem in the *Manyōshū* about Tako.

**44**

*Sanemori:* (story in *Heike Monogatari*, made into Noh play of the same name by Zeami: the word "cruel" in the *haiku* drawn from the Noh) the oldest warrior killed fighting for the Taira clan against the Genji (Minamoto): had dyed his hair black so as not to be spared. Originally, as a young man, had fought for the Genji.

**45**

*Ishiyama:* B lived for some time in the Genjūan on Ishiyama (Stone Mountain) in Ōmi province (cf. *Haikai and Haiku*, p. xiii.).

*no whiter:* white often means transparent in Japanese and is the color of autumn. Spring is blue, summer red, and winter black.

**46**

*Ariake:* evidently B erred, consciously or unconsciously, and intended reference to Arima, 9 mi. from Kobe, upland, famed for its mineral springs. (Cf. opening of the Noh play *Tadanori* for ancient reference.)

*leave kiku unplucked:* cf. *Kiku Jidō* (sometimes known as *Makura Jidō*), Noh play. Recipe for longevity here. The spa water odorous as well as bracing. B dont hide his aches, though he wont exaggerate them either, and his satisfactions also find full breath.

*Teitoku:* (1571–1653) Kyoto-born. Head of Teimon school. Literary scholar, tried to "classicize *haikai* and to return to *renga*" (cf. *Haikai and Haiku*, NGS, p.x.).

*like the parting of a pair of wild geese:* there is a double allusion here—though very personal. B had written a very early *haiku* on the deeply-moving occasion of his young lord Sengin's death (B was possibly still in his teens): "Parting from his friends/A wild goose goes its way/Soon to be beyond the clouds." (clumsy version found in *Haikai and Haiku*, p. 142).

*efface the inscription:* on the *hinoki*-strip hat (*kasa*) pilgrims always had a blessing inscribed: "Between heaven and earth Buddha and I share the journey."

**47**

*sweeping the yard:* B's hasty exit, with appointments in mind, evokes this poem of apology for abruptness. Generally a guest of such a temple would sweep the yard a little in compensation for accommodations. B's sensibility (*fūryū*) indicated by his feeling the "rightness" of the fallen leaves.

**48**

*all night long . . . :* poem attributed to Saigyō; also quoted near the start of the Noh *Yamauba*.

*one finger too many:* suggests *Chuang-tzu,* Bk. VIII, 3. "Webbed toes adding useless flesh to feet, extra fingers planted useless flesh to hands, so over-indulgence, etc."

**49**

*Hokushi:* (1665–1718). Sword-sharpener by trade, became disciple of B on this trip.

*fan wrenched apart . . . .* : the ubiquitous fan would be customarily destroyed at summer's end.

*Dōgenzenji:* (1200–53). Brought Sōtō (Ts'ao-T'ung) Zen into Japan (1253). Studied Zen under Eisai (founder of the Rinzai sect). Went to China in 1223. Built Eiheiji, which Eliot (*op. cit.,* p. 284) calls "the finest monastery in Japan."

**50**

*guidepost:* quite accurate. Actually a branch torn off and stuck in the ground to indicate directions, along by-ways.

**51**

*Yugyō Shōnin:* (Ippen) (1239–1289). Originally Tendai priest, who made much of the Nembutsu (repeated utterance of Buddha's name). Curious dance also part of his evangelical sect. Popularly known by name given here, which means "wandering priest." Cf. the Noh *Yugyō Yanagi.*

**52**

*Suma:* cf. book of that name in the *Genji Monogatari.*

*small shells:* the *masuo (Sanguinolaria elongata Lamarock),* suggesting a poem by Saigyō.

**53**

*Rotsū:* (1651?–1739?). Met B in Edo in 1688. Difficult personality, estranged from B in 1692—but B remained concerned about him.

*Etsujin:* (1656?–1739). An early disciple. An obstinate and irascible man, debating with Shikō literary matters (hierarchy?) after B's death in a series of tracts.

*Jokō:* (?–1706). Former samurai. Priest, disciple.

*Zensenshi:* of Ōgaki, no more known.

*Keikō father and sons:* father (1673–1735). There were 3 sons in fact and all B disciples.

*ceremonial moving at Ise:* the sacred Shinto shrines (especially shrine of Sun-goddess, Ama-terasu: regarded as founder of Japan), a kind of Japanese Mecca. The shrines re-built every twenty years (or in the 21st year), Sept 10–13 by old calendar. B may also here have in mind a *waka* by Saigyō (quoted by Blyth, *op. cit.,* Vol. 2, p. 138), which is a poem of deep gratitude.

*back in the boat again:* referring us to the start of the journal, of the journey.

*clam/shell and innards parting . . . .* : a most difficult poem to bring across, full of inner word-play. The *romaji* goes: *hamaguri-no/futami-ni wakare/yuku aki-zo. futami:* key-word. Place-name of a bay famous for its clams and sunrise seen between rocks. *futa:* "lids" and *-mi:* both "innards" and

**172**

"to see." The shell has opened; B is on the move again. "departing fall" sounds "departing spring" and the breath resumes at a deeper fuller pitch.

BACK ROADS

# FAR TOWNS